God, Why This Evil?

Bruce A. Little

Hamilton Books
A member of
The Rowman & Littlefield Publishing Group
Lanham · Boulder · New York · Toronto · Plymouth, UK

Copyright © 2010 by
Hamilton Books
4501 Forbes Boulevard
Suite 200
Lanham, Maryland 20706
Hamilton Books Acquisitions Department (301) 459-3366

Estover Road
Plymouth PL6 7PY
United Kingdom

Library of Congress Control Number: 2010933268
ISBN: 978-0-7618-5254-4 (paperback : alk. paper)
eISBN: 978-0-7618-5255-1

CONTENTS

PREFACE

This book contains some of the same material contained in my book titled, *A Creation-Order Theodicy: God and Gratuitous Evil*, published by University Press of America (2005). The goal of this present book is to provide a more readable content for the general public. I have attempted remove some of technical language and more detailed historical content. I am not sure how well I actually have achieved this goal but I have tried.

I have written this book because I am more convinced than when I first wrote on this subject that it remains the most common complaint against Christian theism and the most difficult objection to answer. I have spent 30 years of my life before becoming a seminary professor as a pastor of a local church. In this context, I know all too well that it is not only non-Christians who have questions, but Christians as well. Therefore, I trust this volume will provide a clearer presentation of the issues and possible answers for those who seriously wrestle with the different aspects of God and evil.

The purpose of this book is twofold. The first is to give a historical context for understanding the development of how Christianity has traditionally answered the problem of evil. The second is to show the weaknesses of Greater-Good responses which suggest that God only allows the evil in this world from which he can bring about a greater good. The response off here affirms both the providence of God and the existence of gratuitous evil. The proposed response is named the Creation-Order theodicy because it is constructed upon an understanding of divine ordering of creation. This ordering was necessary for the infinite God to have a meaningful relationship with finite man. It established how God would interact with His creation in general and man in particular in lit of the fact that man was given the power of moral choice.

This proposed theodicy owes much to other theologians and philosophers who have wrestled with the argument from evil. The fact remains that any advancement in the understanding of the argument from evil by today's theologians and philosophers owes much to those Christian scholars who have struggled with the problem in the past.

With this debt in mind and full awareness of my own limitations the Creation-Order theodicy is offered as an alternative to the Greater-Good theodicy. If it is right, it is no longer incumbent upon the theist to try to demonstrate that good always comes from all evil/suffering. As Ronald Nash wrote, "If Peterson's observation is correct and if the arguments concerning gratuitous evil in the last few pages are sound, there would seem to be good reason to believe that the stalemate is over and that the probabilities favor theism."[1]

Bruce Little
Wake Forest, North Carolina
March 2010

NOTES

1. Ronald Nash, *Faith and Reason* (Grand Rapids: Zondervan Publishing House, 1988), 221.

ACKNOWLEDGMENTS

I want to express my appreciation for those who have interacted with me on many of the complicated issues regarding the problem of evil over the years. This includes my students as well as some of my colleagues at Southeastern Baptist Theological Seminary. Special thanks to Helen Sharpe and Sarah Sheaffer who read the manuscript and made helpful comments as well as improved the grammatical structure of the manuscript. Finally, I wish to thank the staff at University Press of America who worked with me on bringing this manuscript to light of day. While I am grateful for all the help I have received, I alone bear the responsibility for the content and final format. Any mistakes or shortcomings are mine and mine alone. Unless otherwise noted all quotations from the Bible are taken from the New King James Version of the Bible.

1
THE CASE IN REVIEW

On the clear autumn morning of September 11, 2001, Americans were abruptly confronted by the truth many had desperately endeavored to deny—that evil exists. Stunned by the enormity of the act and the uncertainty of its scope, America briefly acknowledged another discarded truth—the existence of God. In a very small window of recent history, America acknowledged both the existence of evil and the existence of God.

The first was undeniable and the second seemed indispensable, but how the two fit together once again raised the age-old question: If God is all-powerful and all-good, how is it that evil of this magnitude could exist in a world created and maintained by this God? The thought of being all alone in the universe at a time like this was frightening indeed.

For a brief time the nation looked to religion for some explanation of how God fit in all of this mayhem in order that it might have some sense of purpose or, at least, encouragement. Unfortunately, what was heard was a mixture of appeals to mystery, charges of judgment, or promises of some greater good that would obtain because of the evil. In the end, the religious questions abated, and a mantra expressing a secular hope swelled across the land. Disappointed by the religious confusion and theological ambiguity, America turned its hope to rebuilding through a united human effort, thereby abandoning the inquiry about God and His relation to evil. It seemed reasonable that if the Church had no definitive answer to this question of evil, then it was quite possible that man was alone in the universe. It appeared that if one had to choose between acknowledging the reality of one or the other, evil would win, as its reality seemed undeniably based on experience. In the end, this often meant that *the God question* was either dismissed or reserved only for personal religious talk without any correspondence to reality.

While events such as this receive worldwide attention to the suffering of humanity, there are many less-known events every day that offend our moral sensibilities. Consider the little nine-year-old girl who was raped and buried alive or the little five year-old whose head was cut off by her brother at her birthday party or the stories of men killing their family and then taking their own lives. We hear of children killing children over arguments about video games or the volume level of music. In addition, we wonder how it is that a teenage girl can be gang-raped as some 20 bystanders watch and apparently do nothing. Such events beg for some answer, an answer that neither minimizes the horrific nature of the evil, nor simply ignores it by suggesting things like this have always happened. The human heart will not be silent forever on such matters. Furthermore, traditional answers from the well-meaning Christian community are not answering the cry of the heart—God, why this evil?

HOW SOME ANSWER THE QUESTION

The most oft-heard response is that God allowed the evil in order to bring about some greater good[1]. This explanation, now known as the Greater-Good (G-G) Theodicy,[2] is the working model most Christians use to answer questions about evil and suffering. Formally, it states that God allows only the evil from which He can bring about a greater good or prevent a worse evil. This response, I will argue, has not only proven to be unconvincing, but also has in fact committed the theist to a very questionable position that unnecessarily requires him to prove more than is possible.

The existence of evil (or suffering)[3] in a world created by the all-powerful, all-good, all-knowing God[4]appears at first to present both logical and evidential contradictions. If the contradictions were real, they would seemingly make it impossible to reconcile the existence of evil with the existence of this God. This would require the denial of one or the other—or perhaps some redefinition of either or both. Classical theism has viewed these two options as unacceptable. Historically, theists have attempted to offer some justificatory framework by which the existence of the all-knowing, all-powerful, all-good God is reconciled with the existence of evil. The evidential objection (or we can call it an *evidential argument*) claims that with all the evil in the world, it is more likely that God does not exist than that He does exist. Notice that this objection is not an outright denial of God's existence, but in light of all the evil and suffering it is more probable that He does not exist than that He does exist.

Theists, at least since the time of Augustine, have most often responded to the evidential argument from evil by claiming that God is justified in allowing evil because He purposes that through the evil to bring about a greater good or prevent some greater evil. Michael Peterson notes that the "Greater-Good Theodicy is, so to speak, the 'parent', and many particular theodicies are its 'off-spring'."[5] Furthermore, he notes that some notion of the greater good is "integral to their [theists] search for a morally sufficient reason why God allows evil."[6]

G-G theodicies share certain basic tenets, while evidencing diversity with respect to the particulars. For example, they may differ in what should be understood as the good that obtains, or they may give different explanations as to *how* and *when* the good obtains. All of them, however, share two basic tenets that have made them highly susceptible to criticism. The first is that they deny the existence of gratuitous evil.[7] This denial necessarily flows from a particular application of God's sovereignty, which maintains that everything in this life has a purpose precisely because God is sovereign. If any suffering could be determined as pointless (gratuitous), then God must not be sovereign, or so goes the argument, because there would be something outside the sovereign purposes of God. Furthermore, if some good did not obtain, then the greater-good moral justification for God allowing the evil would collapse. However, this seems to confuse the idea of reason and purpose. Something might have a reason, but not necessarily a purpose. For example, if you ask me why I did not pay my electric bill, I might say that it was because I was protesting the recent hike in electric rates—that would be a purpose. On the other hand, I might respond saying that it was because I did not have the money. That would be a reason. I agree there may be overlap, but they are definitely two separate notions. I would maintain that reason is all we need to preserve God's sovereignty and not His purpose.

Clearly, at the heart of G-G theodicies lies the denial of gratuitous evil. In order to sustain this denial, the theist promises that there is always a purpose to all evil in the world—and that purpose is some greater good. This requires the theist to affirm that some greater good obtains in all cases and deny the reality of gratuitous evil in any case. This means the theist must be able to identify the good that comes from the evil.

One can see how difficult is the task in identifying the good that comes from something like the Holocaust. In addition, it must be demonstrated that the good would be great enough to serve as moral justification for God allowing such immense human suffering and pain. In addition, it would need to be shown that the Holocaust was, in fact, necessary for that particular good and it could only obtain as a consequence of the evil. Furthermore, the good would need to be some objective measurement to determine when the good outweighed either qualitatively or quantitatively the evil in terms of human pain and suffering. In the end, one must realize that no objective measure exists, and in addition, there is no way to determine (at least in many cases) the causal relationship between the evil and the good. It is in light of such difficulties that a credibility problem arises for the theist if this is his answer to the existence of evil.

Still, a review of the literature on this subject reveals that this is precisely what theists attempt to do. It is not to say that there may not be situations where one can point to some good following a particular evil, but there is no way to demonstrate that the evil was necessary to the good or that the good outweighed the human suffering and pain. The fact that a good chronologically follows an evil does not prove that it follows because of the evil. It could be a matter of association and not causation.

Furthermore, the greater-good moral justificatory scheme suggests (at least in some cases) that evil might be allowed because by it God prevents a worse evil. However, this creates at least two difficulties for the theist. First, it raises questions about God's omnipotence. If God were omnipotent, He would not be dependent on one evil in order to prevent a worse evil—He could do it by His power. This would make at least some evils necessary to the prevention of other evils. When applied to the Holocaust, for example, one would wonder just what the worse evil might be, but I suppose a worse evil could be imagined.

The second difficulty with this position is that it is meaningless. It is impossible to know whether such a claim is true or not because it deals with a hypothetical. We all know how impossible it is to prove a hypothetical. Someone says, "If I would have married Jane, I would be a millionaire by now." However, how would one know this? He could not. A hypothetical is impossible to prove, unless of course you are God. In the end, it seems that this part of the G-G response is meaningless. Therefore, I will only deal with the greater-good element of this response.

The theist, however, might reply saying that the Bible teaches the G-G response and, therefore, evidential proof is not needed. Of course if this were so, then the matter would be settled. However, it is difficult to find a biblical text that unambiguously teaches any part of the greater-good as a normative response to the question of evil. [8] Remember, I am not suggesting good never comes from evil; I am saying that this response is unsustainable as explaining God's moral justification for the evil. Please note that these are two entirely different matters. This leaves the theist, if I am right, without a propositional statement in the Bible teaching a greater-good response. Later, I will argue what I am only stating here. Therefore, if it is shown that the greater-good response lacks either clear scriptural or evidential support, then it would be time to either reformulate or find a response that did not suffer some clear defeater. At this point, I am only raising possible objections or at least a reasonable doubt as to the theological integrity of the greater-good response. Later in this volume, I will deal with this in detail.

Generally put, whereas the theist claims that God allows *all* evil in this world for the purpose of bringing about a greater good, he must give sufficient reason to conclude that it is so in *every* case. This seems beyond what can be done. Often, the theist, in order to compensate for the lack of evidence, claims that the good does obtain, but humans cannot see it. While it is reasonable to assume that on certain occasions this might be the case, the best it would do is speak to an exception, but say nothing as a rule. If the theist only had to appeal to this argument on rare occasions, then it might be more convincing. Regrettably (for the theist), it is more often than not the case, especially where the suffering is either of gargantuan proportions, such as the Holocaust, or when it involves innocents such as children.[9] The fact is that the empirical evidence that the good always obtains is scarce at best and suspect at worse, and yet it forms a major plank in the greater-good response.

In order for the theist to raise the G-G theodicy to a more defensible posture, he must at least show that in *most* cases the good obtains, especially in situations where the human suffering appears so odious to the moral sensibilities of humanity. Yet, it is precisely such episodes in the human experience that the theist must confess that he cannot produce the evidence that the good always obtains. Of course, under the right circumstances, it would be admissible for the theist to move to a deductive argument—God is sovereign, therefore the good *must* obtain. However, this is an inferential argument and the task here is to explain why the sovereignty of God requires such a conclusion. It will be argued later in this volume, however, that such an inference is not necessarily a correct inference.

THE OCCASION FOR THE ARGUMENT

It is not the existence of evil in and of itself, but the fact that evil exists in a world created by the all-good, all-powerful Christian God that creates the moral dilemma for the theist. According to C. S. Lewis, the claim that God exists "creates rather than solves the problem of pain, for pain would be no problem unless, side by side with our daily experience of this painful world, we had received what we think a good assurance that ultimate reality is righteous and loving."[10] Or as Vladimir Lossky writes, "Evil as a problem thus stems necessarily from Christianity."[11] Furthermore, it is not that there is *some* evil in the world that gives rise to the argument from evil, but that there is so much suffering. Often, the human experience painfully reminds us that suffering tends to be unequally distributed as well as often it is the innocent and the righteous who suffer. That innocent children suffer was precisely the point made by Fyodor Dostoevsky in *The Brothers Karamazov* and Albert Camus in *The Plague*. One also finds the perplexing phenomena of the righteous suffering a point made repeatedly in the Bible. It is the reality of the all-pervasiveness of human suffering that urges the theist to explain how God is morally justified in permitting the continuance of such suffering in the world of which He is both creator and sustainer. In so many cases, such horrific suffering has all the appearance of being without purpose or in other words—gratuitous.

In fact, David Basinger points out that gratuitous evil seems to be the most difficult issue within the evidential argument from evil.[12] Peterson writes with agreement, "The evidential argument from gratuitous evil is now widely considered the most formidable objection to theistic belief."[13] The primary reason gratuitous evil is so formidable is that most theodicies deny gratuitous evil and yet there is no observable evidence to support the claim. Theists simply deny that gratuitous evil exists by contending that certain evils only 'appear' to be gratuitous. This position flows from the assumption that God is all-knowing, all-good and all-powerful, and that His sovereign providence insures that everything that happens in His creation has its divine purpose. That would mean that in the case of human choice, the choice would serve the purposes of God— such as the choice to rape and bury alive a little nine-year old girl. The question that remains, however, is whether classical theism as a whole necessarily requires the theist to deny gratuitous evil in order to preserve God's ontological integrity and sovereignty. In the pages that follow, I will argue that it is neither theologically necessary nor philosophically inconsistent to claim gratuitous evil exists while affirming that God is all-knowing, all-good, all-powerful, and sovereign.

THE FORM OF THE ARGUMENT

Traditionally, there have been two versions of *the argument from evil*. One is the logical and the other is the evidential. The logical problem states that it is logically impossible that God exists. The argument is framed in the following way:

    A. God is all-good; He would destroy all evil

    B. God is all-powerful; He could destroy all evil

    C. Evil exists

    Therefore, God does not exist.

The argument here is that there is a logical inconsistency within the three-member set. That is, one could affirm A and C, or B and C, but not A, B, and C and remain logically consistent. However, Alvin Plantinga points out that there is no explicit or implicit logical inconsistency. He puts forth an argument that he believes shows there is not even an implicit contradiction. With this argument, many think Plantinga has defeated the logical argument. Whether or not Plantinga has defeated the logical argument from evil is not the point of concern here. The focus throughout these pages is on the evidential argument as that is the objection most often encountered in everyday conversation.

    The evidential argument does seem as a rather convincing argument against God, at least in terms of human experience. It claims that in light of the kind and extent of suffering in this world, it is more likely that God does not exist than He does exist. It is not only the volume of horrific suffering caused by evil intentions of moral agents, but that human suffering seems so unequally distributed. Particularly troubling is the suffering of small children. Furthermore, it seems that most often there is little or no connection between the kind of life a person lives and the suffering that person experiences. One can think of the children who suffer because of the evil deeds of parents or politicians. Their suffering seems so senseless, so purposeless that the intuitive cry of the heart asks the *"Why"* question. If the moral structure of our universe was such that there was always some purpose in the suffering, just because that was the way reality is, then the human heart would not ask that question, at least not in the way it asks the question. When we throw a ball up in the air and it returns to the earth, we do not ask why even if we knew nothing of the concept of gravity—we simply knew, intuitively, because that is the way the universe is structured physically. Of course, one might ask in a curious way, that is, to understand how the structure of the universe works, but that is not the same kind of a *why question* that arises when we are faced with evil. Human beings seem to have an intuitive sense about the way the universe is structured. I suggest the same would be so with evil and suffering. If there was always a divine (or otherwise) purpose because of the moral structure of the universe, we would know it to be that way. At least I think this raises a legitimate question, even if those reading this are at first skeptical of this point. I should say, however, that this point is not essential to the argument presented in this volume, even though I think the point is legitimate.

At the heart of the question regarding evil is whether the evil that appears gratuitous is, in fact, gratuitous. This is not to say all evil, but only that *some* evil might be gratuitous. If some evil is gratuitous in actuality and not only in appearance, the question would be whether that would count conclusively against God's sovereignty and goodness? If it did, then for no other reason than this, it seems the Christian theist would have to deny the existence of gratuitous evil. However, is it possible that gratuitous evil exists and it does not count against the moral character of God? As Edward Madden and Peter Hare suggest, "The really interesting problem of evil is whether the apparent gratuity can be explained away by more ingenious measures or whether the gratuity is real and hence detrimental to religious belief."[14] The fundamental assumption of G-G theodicies is that if gratuitous evil exists, it would seriously challenge the claim that an all-good, all-powerful, all-knowing, sovereign God exists. Adherents of G-G theodicies claim gratuitous evil does not exist because it cannot exist; as they see it, the existence of gratuitous evil would render meaningless the very attributes of God that are essential to God. If gratuitous evil exists, they argue, God is neither all-powerful nor sovereign over His creation. This is not a logical misstep for the theist, for often we find an explanation for a particular phenomenon, which in turn justifies the initial premise. The point being made in this volume is simply that this is not the only possible conclusion, nor is it the only understanding of sovereignty. In fact, it is precisely one of the more crucial points of this volume; that is, gratuitous evil can be admitted without it counting against the character of God, as traditionally understood within classical theism (this includes God's sovereignty). For clarification, when I speak of classical theism, I must make it clear that I do so while denying the theological position known as *open theism*.[15]

A further point to be made is that it seems that the theist's greater-good response has unintended consequences. By that I mean it actually strengthens the atheist's claim. By grounding the argument in the assumption that God is morally justified in permitting evil in this world only because from it He brings a greater good, places the onus squarely on the theist to prove that a greater good obtains (at least in most cases). Not only that it actually obtains, but the good would not occur unless the evil also occurred. For if the good could obtain by some other means (even a lesser evil), then it seems that the all-good God would allow the alternative means of the good. This presents itself as a rather daunting, if not impossible task on evidential grounds, or so it seems to me. In fact, in most cases it is impossible to demonstrate with any degree of certainty or even beyond reasonable doubt. Therefore, in the absence of unambiguous evidence from human experience, it seems that the atheist's objection maintains its force in that it appears the Christian response is actually no response at all.

The existence of evil, however, does not require a Christian to give up his belief that God exists, nor his personal commitment to God. It may be that he has other counterbalancing reasons for belief in God. Nonetheless, the existence of evil still requires a response. It is part of this world, and as Christians, our theology is not only about the world to come, but this world as well. Part of this world—yes, even a large part, is made up of human suffering. If God is there, how is it that He allows so much human suffering when it seems so contrary to His good purposes for humanity? And, I want to be clear that if something happens in God's creation it is because He has allowed it. Surely, this requires some coherent response from the Christian world.

Christians claim that the Christian worldview answers the questions of life better and more consistently than another belief system. Therefore, in keeping with this claim, Christians must be prepared to give a sustainable biblical answer to the critic or the atheist regarding his objection to theism on the grounds of evil. In the end, this is an interpretative issue as we are all looking at the same facts and trying to find the best explanation that fits all the facts consistently. As it is so often the case, the problem does not lie in the facts of the case. Rather, in the explanatory system constructed to interpret the facts that we think lead to the best explanation.

In addition to the concerns already raised, there are theological implications associated with the G-G theodicy. For example, is the good a *necessary good* (that is, necessary to the plan of God) or only an *incidental good*? If it is a necessary good, can that good be obtained apart from the evil from which it comes? If the good is necessary and logically bound to the evil, then it logically follows that the evil is also necessary. This raises questions of God's relationship to and dependence on evil for certain goods in this world. That is, does God need evil to accomplish some good? And, if more good makes a better world, then does it logically follow that more evil is actually better, as in each case the good outweighs the evil, making a net gain of good? Furthermore, how should one understand the purpose of the Incarnation—did Jesus really come to destroy evil? If so, it seems that evil is really contrary to the will and plan of God.

Or, consider the question of social justice. If evil is necessary to the good, should Christians attempt to stop evil? If certain evils are stopped, would that mean that certain goods would never obtain? Maybe more troubling is that G-G theodicies logically lead to the conclusion that God is responsible for evil. These are only a few of the questions that must be—and will be—considered in judging the theological implications of G-G theodicies and, hence, their theological integrity as well as their practical sufficiency.

WHAT IS THE ARGUMENT?

Theistic proposals for solving the problem of evil develop in response to objections raised by proponents of atheism.[16] In order to determine the adequacy of a theistic response, it will be helpful to review one of the most significant objections to theism as formed by a noted atheist. William Rowe[17] crafts an evidential argument that appears to be a very strong argument against God in general and against the G-G theodicy in particular.[18] A look at this argument provides an example of how an atheist might form his objection to God's existence based on the presence of evil in this world. Remember, this argument does not say God cannot exist, but only that it seems more likely that he does not exist than he does exist. By introducing this example from Rowe it is not suggesting that this argument is compelling or that it is not without weaknesses. What it does is gives a real and fair objection as put forth by one who calls himself a *friendly atheist*.

Rowe presents his objection to theism by focusing on the inductive approach to the evidential problem of evil, arguing that theism lacks plausibility in light of evil. Rowe centers his evidential argument on what he takes to be the reality of gratuitous evil. He argues:

> The latest formulation I have given of the evidential problem of evil goes something like this. (E 1 is the case of a fawn trapped in a forest fire and undergoing several days of terrible agony before dying. E 2 is the case of the rape, beating, and murder by strangulation of a five-year-old girl).
>
> P: No good we know of justifies an omnipotent, omniscient, perfectly good being in permitting E 1 and E 2;
>
> therefore,
>
> Q: No good at all justifies an omnipotent, omniscient, perfectly good being in permitting E 1 and E 2;
>
> therefore,
>
> not-G: there is no omnipotent, omniscient, perfectly good being.[19]

He begins by pointing out what he is and is not saying. Concerning *P* he asks, "What counts as a 'good that we know of?' I do not mean to limit us to goods that we know to have occurred. Nor do I mean to limit us to those goods and goods that we know will occur in the future."[20] Bound up in the notion of 'goods' is anything past, present or future, even something like God rewarding someone in His kingdom. The only stipulation that Rowe places on the good is that in order for it to count as a good, it must be actual. He also suggests that the non-existence of God would be sufficient reason for affirming *P* as true.

What Rowe does not allow into the discussion is what he calls *background information k*. There can be no evidence outside the reality of evil to tip the scales, such as the enormous amount of evil (this would support the atheist position) or order in the universe (this would support the theist position—this would include theistic arguments). That is, *k* by itself can neither make "God's existence nor His nonexistence more likely than not."[21] Conversely, if *P* appears to be true and, consequently, "lowers the probability of God's existence, it is open to the theist to reply that the addition to *k* of other information concerning the occurrences of ordinary and mystical religious experiences restores the balance or even tips the scales in favor of theism."[22] What Rowe says is that it is possible that a person "might have stronger evidence for the existence of God than is provided by the problem of evil for the nonexistence of God."[23] This, however, would be personal or existential evidence that only has weight for the individual and has no influence in the discussion of the public debate on the problem of evil.

With this in place, Rowe develops his inductive argument, concluding that there is no sufficient reason to believe that there is any good knowable to man that would justify God permitting E 1 and E 2. Note, he is not saying there may be no good, but there is no good known to man that would *justify* God permitting these evils. This is, of course, as long as the definition of God remains as the all-good, all-knowing and all-powerful God. His point follows that even if one accepts the good of E 2 to be Sue's enjoyment of the presence of God forever, an all-good, all-powerful God would find a better way to accomplish that good. He even answers a response that suggests that God allowed Sue to die because, had she lived, she would have hardened her heart against the Lord and been shut out of His presence forever. Rowe quickly, and correctly, points out that this runs counter to the notion of free will, which is a foundational plank of the theist's position on the presence of evil in the world. He concludes, "Given our common knowledge of the evils and goods in our world and our reasons for believing that *P* is true, it is *irrational* to believe in theism unless we possess or discover strong evidence in its behalf. I conclude, therefore, that the evidential argument from evil is alive and well."[24]

Rowe's argument seems to raise some serious questions for those who are committed to the premise of G-G theodicies. Although Alston thinks that Rowe's formulation of the problem "is the most careful and perspicuous,"[25] he is sure that the theist's position will prevail. While Alston thinks maybe he has answered Rowe's question sufficiently, just in case all are not convinced, he comforts himself with a common retreat: "Even if we were fully entitled to dismiss all the alleged reasons for permitting suffering that have been suggested, we would still have to consider whether there are further possibilities that are undreamt of in our theodicies. Why should we suppose that the theodicies thus far excogitated, however brilliant and learned their authors, exhaust the field?"[26]

In fact, Alston thinks this is a very convincing position, for he says the skeptic would still "face the insurmountable task of showing herself to be justified in supposing that there are no other possibilities for sufficient divine reasons. That point by itself would be decisive."[27] In other words, even if the theist's response has not answered all the questions at this point, it does not mean that fuller and more satisfying answers may not be forthcoming in the future. Therefore, the theist should not be concerned that all objections have not been answered.

While it is true that in time a more satisfying theistic response to the argument for evil may be developed, it seems unwise for the theist to take comfort in that position. After all, if the G-G theodicy is theologically legitimate, then it should be able to answer the questions now. What this reveals is that the G-G theodicy is an inadequate framework from which to construct a response to the evidential argument from evil. Alston is right on one point, namely that the G-G theodicy does not answer all the questions. This being true,

I believe this signals the need not for more answers from exhausted G-G theodicies but rather a new paradigm altogether.

UNDERSTANDING THE CHALLENGE FOR A NEW THEODICY

Theists currently involved in the work of theodicy generally agree that the argument from evil has yet to receive a sufficient answer, and understandably so as it is a most difficult task. Richard Swinburne suggests that "in the West in our modern world, most theists need a theodicy. Without a theodicy, evil counts against [our belief in and understanding of] the existence of God."[28] Swinburne suggests that evil weighs against theism as a consistent system, unless the theist has a theodicy. Furthermore, the complexity of developing a satisfactory theodicy is highlighted by Swinburne's own confession. He points out that even though he had addressed the subject earlier[29] he admits "that theodicy is a considerably more difficult enterprise than I represented it there."[30] Millard Erickson also suggests that theodicy has not yet finished its work. In his discussion on the importance of the doctrine of God, he says, "The problem of evil, of course, is a major and, indeed, perhaps the largest, problem for any theism."[31] Erickson suggests that the coming theological debates will include discussions of the problem of evil, which he thinks may very well be the greatest problem for theists.

The appearance of several recent books[32] dealing with the subject of *theodicy* indicates that the argument from evil has not yet been put to rest. The fact that the issue continues to receive serious attention by theologians and philosophers alike indicates that a convincing and coherent theodicy has yet to be developed.[33] In addition, while much has been done in developing convincing arguments for God's existence, responses to the argument from evil have not fared as well. Some might argue that this is to be expected for the ways of God in this matter are a mystery, hidden from the eyes of the mortal. While there is no disagreement that there are matters belonging to God alone, in light of biblical record and human experience, evil seems to be not one of those matters. If it is, there is a very large hole in Christian theology.

It is the human experience that begs for some answer, some meaningful clarification. It is the pervasiveness of evil and the personal affliction from evil that causes the heart to cry: "God, why this evil?" I would suggest that more Christians than one would acknowledge are dissatisfied with the standard fare from preachers on the questions from evil, whether it relates to their personal lives, ministering to others, understanding suffering in general, or trying to answer the skeptic. Most Christians, however, resist complaining publicly lest their faith be questioned by other Christians. Although some become bitter towards God in the midst of their suffering, most simply experience a reduced confidence in God. While the majority will continue to believe in God, they sense disappointment because they search in vain to find the good from suffering experienced by either themselves or one they love. Consequently, it must be clear that the demand for a more satisfactory theodicy goes beyond a philosophical quest, and it is more than just satisfying one's curiosity. It is about answering the silent (or muffled) request from the hearts of multitudes of Christians. It is the painful cry of the heart, "Where's the good?" Often, the simple reply of the preacher, "It is there; you just cannot see it" fails to heal the soul deep down.

When evaluating the importance of a theodicy, one must understand that a theodicy serves at least two important functions. One is to answer the objections brought by the atheist who thinks that evil is a defeater of any claim for belief in God. Most, when thinking about theodicy, think of it only in these terms. There remains, however, another important function of a theodicy; namely, to serve as a platform from which the Christian understands his own encounters with suffering. Those who would suggest that theodicy is a poor use of one's time and energy should understand that without a theodicy, comforting those who suffer has no enduring foundation. Effective Christian ministering to those who are suffering requires proper understanding of the relationship of suffering to God. As Peterson claims, "Thus, it is quite legitimate for theists to try to formulate some reasonable understanding of evil for themselves, and whatever understanding they obtain moves them in the direction of theodicy."[34] Furthermore, it is essential that any theodicy not only answer the particular problem of evil, but at the same time show consistency with all other Christian truth claims concerning creation and God's character. Consequently, it is necessary within a Christian theistic worldview to develop a theodicy as part of the Christian belief system.

It logically follows that, if God works within the space-time context (which now contains evil), to avoid providing an explanation for the existence of evil in God's creation seems to leave a part of the space-time reality outside the Christian worldview. Such a position would have serious implications for the reality of miracles and other acts of God, such as the Incarnation and Resurrection of Jesus the Christ. Trinitarian theism most often affirms miracles (God working in the space-time context), which deal (directly or indirectly) with the problem of evil. Furthermore, much of the biblical text either explicitly or tacitly deals with evil. To suggest that there is no explanation for why God allowed evil in this world and while He continues to permit much horrific evil is to say that much of what happens in space-time is unexplainable.[35] Logically, another possibility would be to conclude that God does not work in the space-time context.[36] In either case, what would be left is a God that looks very much like a Deistic God, not the Trinitarian God of the Bible. The theme of God dealing with evil runs throughout the Bible; therefore, it seems reasonable to assume there is sufficient information on which a theodicy can be constructed. Furthermore, as Peterson points out, most theists have not considered a theodicy impossible. He writes

> Rather, they [theists] conceive of the project of theodicy as drawing out the implications of one's theological position from evil. After all, religious believers commonly accept that the doctrines and teaching of their faith have implications for all sorts of important matters—moral and spiritual virtues, the

meaning of redemption, the purpose of human life, and so forth. So, it would be odd indeed to think that religious beliefs have no implications whatsoever for understanding something so important as evil in the world.[37]

If one avoids an attempt to explain why God allows evil, he will have to face implications for understanding miracles when the choice to avoid explanation runs to its logical end. Therefore, I would maintain that answers to questions of evil are necessary to a total Christian theistic worldview.

Furthermore, the problem of evil, as discussed by contemporary scholars, is both tacitly and explicitly bound up in the renewed discussion of the nature of God as Trinity. That is not to say that the discussion of evil has been responsible for the renewed interest in the nature of God, only that it is related to the discussion on the problem of evil. Presently, issues such as the impassibility of God, the eternality of God, the omniscience of God, and the omnipotence of God are often being reviewed in light of the problem of evil.[38]

It seems reasonable to conclude that if evil exists as a reality in this world and this is God's creation, then there must be some explanation for its continued existence—an explanation that is compatible with God as God. While it is true that the Cross event is God's means of ultimately destroying evil, it is only a future reality. The question before us is why God allows the pervasive and destructive evil in His world now. God does not ask mankind to believe that which stands in contradiction to His character, nor does He hide His working among men. To deny the possibility of a theodicy is to leave much of the biblical material outside an understandable Christian worldview.

As already mentioned, historically the Christian community has answered the problem of evil by appealing to some form of a G-G theodicy. As Peterson points out, "Most theodicies therefore follow the strategy of specifying either greater goods that are gained or worse evils that are averted by God's permitting evil."[39] As such, most theodicies have a common theme running through them, namely that "*God (who is omnipotent, omniscient, and wholly good) would design the universe such that evil is necessary to a greater good.* Theists have typically taken a *greater-good approach* as integral to their search for a morally sufficient reason for why God allows evil."[40] The Evangelical[41]consensus seems to be that maybe no one version of the G-G theodicy answers all the questions, but it is still the best we have. I, however, would argue that settling for what is known to be less than satisfactory is an unacceptable theological position to hold and, instead, we should revisit the issue to see if a better answer could be found. It is to this end that this volume is dedicated. Not that it will be the final answer, but that it presents a different way of looking at the question to see if that would yield a more promising answer.

CLARIFICATION OF TERMS

Many controversies arise, in part, because of either a lack of precision in definitions or no attention given to definitions. Important to any meaningful discussion is a mutual understanding of key terms or concepts used in the discussion. Although there may not be complete agreement with the definitions given, the purpose here is to inform the reader with the definitions of words/concepts as used in this book. At the very least, this should minimize confusion even if it does not produce complete agreement. It is believed, however, that the definitions given here follow an orthodox understanding of the terms.

Free will

This term carries baggage that proves unnecessarily confusing and requires too many qualifications in order to convey its exact meaning. Therefore, the term/phrase of choice here will be *libertarian freedom*. To affirm that the will is free is difficult to defend, if used in an absolute sense. In general, *libertarian freedom* as used here means that man has the power to choose to the contrary, and in doing so has the power to cause events. It acknowledges that antecedent choices and events may influence and/or limit present or future choices. In some cases, such choices may determine an unalterable course of events which cannot be reversed by another choice, such as jumping out of a window on the thirtieth floor of an apartment building. Libertarian freedom, however, maintains that man has the ability to make authentic choices from the options permitted within his circumstances and God's providence. His choices may be limited, but not his ability to choose. There are times when his choices are other than they would be under different circumstances (as when there is a gun to your head in conjunction with a command to give the gun-holder your wallet), or his choices may be limited, yet he still has the ability itself to choose. Even when there is a gun to your head, you still have a choice. Consider that Christians have often been called upon to choose the unnatural simply in obedience to Christ.

The word "choice" implies two things; in order for choice to be authentic, there must be at least two possibilities that are equal in possibility, but not necessarily in desirability or workability. For example, one may require more energy or sacrifice. Furthermore, there must be corollary consequences for each choice. When taken as a whole, libertarian freedom affirms that God has given man true ability to choose between two or more possibilities where man can refrain from one and choose the other. Authentic possibilities from which to choose require moral judgment, which is part of libertarian freedom. From each choice, certain consequences follow. The consequences may vary, may be direct or indirect, immediate or delayed, and may affect the individual as well as others, but consequences do follow. Man is morally accountable for those choices; that is, he bears a moral responsibility.

Good

The concept of *good* has two definitions. One can speak of *good* in the intrinsic sense. For example, when one says that God is good, the meaning is that whatever else God is, the quality of goodness is always present in his character. Furthermore, even though God's ways are not our ways (Is. 55:8), His view of what is good may not always be clearly understood by man, but it is never contrary to *good* as revealed in God's word. As Lewis writes, "If God's moral judgment differs from ours so that our 'black' may be His 'white,' we can mean nothing by calling Him good; for to say 'God is good,' while asserting that His goodness is wholly other than ours, is really only to say 'God is we know not what.' And an utterly unknown quality in God cannot give us moral grounds for loving and obeying Him."[42] Therefore, the fact that "God's ways are not our ways" is not justification for using the term *good* equivocally.

The other definition involves *good* in the sense of something being favorable in a relative sense. That is, S is a favorable state of affairs from the perspective of X; however, from the perspective of Y, it could be an unfavorable state of affairs. For example, it is good for John that he arrived at the store in time to purchase the last Skill Saw on sale. However, it is not good for Paul that John arrived when he did because he also needed the Skill Saw. In this case, *good* is not something intrinsic to the act. It would not be *good* from both the perspective of X and Y. However, this is an example of *good* being a relative evaluative term entirely, in that a certain happening appears favorable to or consistent with an individual's particular desires or needs.

Omnipotence

God is Himself and not His opposite. God cannot violate His own nature, and thus He cannot do the logically impossible. The law of non-contradiction does not stand above or apart from God, but rather issues from the essence of God. This law expresses something of the true nature of ultimate reality—a thing is what it is and not something else. Therefore, to say that the law of non-contradiction binds God is not to imply that there is something greater than God to which God is a servant. It simply means that the perfection of God's reality is of such a quality that He is not capable of doing that which entails a logical contradiction of Himself. To do so would result in some violence to the harmony of His essence or, in fact, be destructive to it. As Lewis correctly observes,

> meaningless combinations of words do not suddenly acquire meaning simply because we prefix to them the two other words, "God can." It remains true that all *things* are possible with God: the intrinsic impossibilities are not things but nonentities. It is no more possible for God than for the weakest of His creatures to carry out both of two mutually exclusive alternatives; not because His power meets an obstacle, but because nonsense remains nonsense even when we talk about God.[43]

Therefore, the problem of evil cannot be answered by arguing in any way that God does the logically impossible. Nor can God be charged with being less than omnipotent on grounds that He cannot act contrary to the law of non-contradiction. It would be like saying that God is not omnipotent because He cannot lie or make a rock so heavy He cannot lift it. It must be pointed out, on the other hand, that God is not bound to do something just because it is logically possible for Him to do it. When the Bible says that with God all things are possible, it is always within the context of what has just been promised (Luke 1:37). All things God has promised he can do, and God can do all things consistent with His character.

Omniscience

The knowledge of God is understood to be without limits within the range of what is logically possible for God to know. This means that God's knowledge is not limited by scope or kind, only by quality. God cannot know that which is counter to the facts of actuality or potentiality. For example, God cannot know that a being is a boy and a non-boy at the same time, same place, and in the same way. God's knowledge does, however, encompass the true *actual* as well as the true *potential*; that means He has knowledge of all past, present and future realities. The difference is that the true *actual* is the event itself actualized, while the true *potential* deals only with what might be under different circumstances whether or not it is ever actualized. God's omniscience includes middle knowledge in which God knows all true counterfactuals.

Furthermore, if God knows all things, it means He must know things He has not determined. If God can only know that which He has determined, either all things are determined or there are some things that God does not know (at least prior to their happening). If all things are determined, then *libertarian freedom* is non-authentic and the foundation of all theodicies since Augustine is destroyed. If, however, God does not know all things, then He is not omniscient. The only lack of knowledge that would not count against God's omniscience would be knowledge that is logically impossible for God to know.

But what kind of knowledge might this be? Some have suggested that it is the knowledge associated with the future choices of His moral agents.[44] This, however, seems hard to maintain logically. For example, are there cases where God claims to know some future choices of His moral agents? Consider the case of the people mentioned in Revelation 11:10, where in speaking of a future event, God proclaims He knows what these people will choose to do after killing the two witnesses—they will "rejoice over them, make merry, and send gifts to one another." Clearly, these are independent future choices of moral beings. If God can know in one case the future choices of His moral agents, then there are no logical grounds on which to argue such knowledge is logically impossible for God to know. Since God knows such knowledge, it must be logically possible. It appears that God can know things He has not determined, which means that all His knowledge is not causal. Therefore, the view of omniscience here is that God knows all things (events/happenings mental and overt) at which point they were logically knowable. That is, God could not know that He *had* created a world before the world was created (contingent knowledge) although He could always *know* (natural knowledge) that He would create a world.

Also, God knows all essential Truth or what might be called *natural knowledge* or *necessary knowledge*. By this it is affirmed that God knows all that is true concerning Truth itself in the absolute sense and in this sense God never acquires knowledge. Such knowledge is not knowledge about what happens; this is knowledge in its essential state by which all other propositions and formation of all authentic propositions are judged.

Providence

Providence is about God's governance of creation in a personal and daily way. When God delivered the Israelites from Egypt through the crossing of the Red Sea, that was God's providential work. It is God doing something that otherwise would not have happened with nature left to itself. It is not always clear when God intervenes, although it is clear He can as He wishes, but always with a purpose. If everything, however, is determined, then there is no place for providence. In fact, if everything is determined, there is no need for providence, for what is, is what was determined. I think it is safe to say that miracles are examples of God's providential involvement in creation. Although the universe has a moral and physical structure or ordering, God's providence works within that ordering, but never contrary to it. It is true that certain miracles seem to go against the ordering of the universe, but that view is the result of imprecise thinking. What a miracle does is overturns what sin and corruption have done to creation, such as the Resurrection. Death is not part of the initial ordering of the universe; it is the consequence of sin (Ro 5:12). The moral and physical ordering are the normal way of creation working, but it is always subject to the One who constantly holds it together (Col 1; Heb 1). Furthermore, when something like this happens, it is always local and specific; it is not universal and general. What is not possible is the changing of the ordering that is core to or intrinsic to creation, such as the law of non-contradiction. Providence cannot intervene and make a circle square and it still be a circle.

When something happens that surprises us, that is an event that turns out differently than expected or an event goes differently than what is regular. A man is driving down the highway and in front of him is a vehicle towing an earth-moving machine on a trailer. There is a malfunction in the hitch, the trailer comes loose and slams into the vehicle, killing the driver. Now normally that does not happen. It is not the event itself that surprises us, but the timing of the event. Often people will say "It was meant to be." It is their way of explaining the timing of the event. The event is totally explainable in terms of physics. There is no mystery there. The explanation of the time of the event leads people to say it was meant to be; that, however, raises the question of who meant it to be and why was it was meant to be. Those questions often are not addressed or even asked. But we must ask them if that is going to be our explanation.

World

As we shall see later, Leibniz taught that this is the best of all possible worlds. I agree. Before you close this book in disbelief over what I just said, hear what is meant by the word *world*. By this I mean all that is included from creation to re-creation in the eschaton. That is, when I use the word *world*, I do not mean just what is at this time, but what the world was and will be in the Kingdom. So often when we say there could have been a better world, we mean the way things are at the moment. But that would be an unfortunate use of the word *world*. The world is God's creation as well as its history. There is continuity from creation to re-creation, and hence, I will use the word *world* to speak of that entire continuum and not just what is happening at some particular point of time.

NOTES

1.   The idea of the 'greater good' can be understood in at least two ways. The first is a greater good with reference to the state of affairs before evil came into existence. In this case, the greater good is measured against what was prior to evil, which makes the conditions prior to evil a 'greater good' than the evil that came about as a result of the good state of affairs. This good state of affairs is most often described as the fact that man was given the libertarian freedom commonly referred to as *free will*. The second way to understand the term is where 'greater good' is in reference to the evil; that is, what happens is in some way better than the evil state of affairs out of which it comes. This helpful distinction was made by William Hasker, who credits William Rowe for calling the two notions to his attention. See William Hasker, "The Necessity of Gratuitous Evil," *Faith and Philosophy* 9 (Jan 1992): 40.

2.   Robert Adams "Theodicy" in *The Cambridge Dictionary of Philosophy* (1995), notes that the term 'theodicy' is "from Greek *theos,* 'God' and *dikē,* 'justice'. Michael Peterson, *God and Evil* (Boulder, CO: Westview Press, 1998), 85 explains that it is "as John Milton says, an attempt to 'justify the ways of God to man.'" The term itself appears to be first used by Gottfried Wilhelm Leibniz (1646–1716).

3.   The terms 'evil' and 'suffering' will be used interchangeably. The word 'evil' is not being used in a strict theological sense, but rather in the sense that whatever is named *evil* is something that causes suffering and that all suffering is in some way related to evil, but not necessarily evil itself. For example, suffering is sometimes caused by God's judgment, but one would not call that *moral evil*, even though it does mean suffering. Nonetheless, it is related to evil, namely the evil of immorality.

4.   From this point forward, the term 'God' or 'theism' is used to speak of God in a restricted way that includes the idea that God is omnipotent, omniscient, eternal, and omni-benevolent or a belief in the existence of such a Trinitarian God who acts in space and time.

5.   Michael Peterson, *God and Evil* (Boulder, CO: Westview Press, 1998), 89.

6.   Ibid., 103.

7. 'Gratuitous evil' is evil which causes unnecessary or pointless suffering. That is, it is evil that appears so excessive (both in terms of extent and/or intensity) that it seems inexplicable in terms of any greater good, particularly when the one suffering is innocent, such as a child burning to death. 'Gratuitous evil' is evil that not only *appears* pointless, but is in *reality* pointless.

8. I realize that immediately some will think of Romans 8:28, and understandably so. The most that one can get from this text (and it may be more than the text actually yields, which will be discussed later) is that the good obtains for the Christian only. Therefore, it cannot be applied universally to all suffering, and would not support a theodicy.

9. When I speak of children being innocent, I am not suggesting they are not corrupted from birth. I am not using the word in its theological sense, but rather in a sense of personal moral culpability for personal actions.

10. C. S Lewis, *The Problem of Pain* (New York: Macmillan, 1962; reprint, New York: Simon & Schuster, 1996), 12–13 (page citations are to the reprint edition).

11. Vladimir Lossky, *Orthodox Theology: An Introduction*, trans. Ian and Ihita Kesarcodi-Watson, (Crestwood, NY: St. Vladimir's Seminary Press, 1989), 79.

12. David Basinger, *The Case For Freewill Theism* (Downers Grove: InterVarsity Press, 1996), 83.

13. Peterson, *God and Evil*, 85.

14. Edward Madden and Peter Hare, *Evil and the Concept of God* (Springfield, IL: Charles C. Thomas Publisher, 1968), 3.

15. *Open theism* teaches that God knows all past and present events and choices of his moral agents, but He does not know the future choices of his moral agents.

16. When speaking of *atheism*, it should be noted that the word often is used in two different ways. One is to refer to a person who believes God does not exist. We might call this *hard atheism*. The second use refers to a person who personally does not believe in God. We might call this *soft atheism* or maybe just speak of this person as an unbeliever. In this volume, I have in mind primarily the hard atheist.

17. William Rowe, "The Evidential Argument from Evil: A Second Look," in *The Evidential Argument From Evil*, ed. Daniel Howard-Snyder (Bloomington: Indiana University Press, 1996).

18. For those who would like to see other atheistic responses, they can be found in my book, *A Creation-Order Theodicy: God and Gratuitous Evil* (chapters 3-4).

19. Rowe, "The Evidential Argument from Evil: A Second Look," 262-63.

20. Ibid., 264.

21. Ibid., 265.

22. Ibid., 266.

23. Ibid.

24. Ibid., 282.

25. William Alston, "The Inductive Argument from Evil and the Human Condition," in *The Evidential Argument from Evil*, ed. Daniel Howard-Snyder (Bloomington: Indiana University Press, 1996), 98.

26. Ibid., 119.

27. Ibid.

28. Richard Swinburne, *Providence and the Problem of Evil* (Oxford: Clarendon Press, 1998), x.

29. See Richard Swinburne, *The Existence of God*, rev. ed. (Oxford: Clarendon Press, 1991), 200-224.
30. Swinburne, *Providence and the Problem of Evil*, x.
31. Millard Erickson, *God, the Father Almighty* (Grand Rapids: Baker Book House, 1998), 288.
32. Some of the recent books on evil include William A. Dembski, *The End of Christianity: Finding a Good God in an Evil World* (Nashville: B&H Publishing Group, 2009); Udo Middelmann, *The Innocence of God* (Colorado Springs: Paternoster Publishing, 2007); Peter van Inwagen, *The Problem of Evil: The Gifford Lectures Delivered in the University of St. Andrews in 2003* (New York: Oxford University Press, USA, 2006); N.T. Wright, *Evil and the Justice of God* (Downers Grove: InterVarsity Press, 2006); D.Z. Phillips, *The Problem of Evil and the Problem of God* (Minneapolis: Augsburg Fortress Publishers, 2005); Peter Van Inwagen, *Christian Faith and The Problem of Evil* (Grand Rapids: Wm. B. Eerdmans Publishing Company, 2004); Cornelius G. Hunter, *Darwin's God: Evolution And The Problem Of Evil* (Ada, MI: Brazos Press, 2001); Gregory A. Boyd, *Satan and the Problem of Evil* (Downers Grove: InterVarsity Press, 2001); William L. Rowe, ed., *God and the Problem of Evil* (Malden, MA: Blackwell Publishers, Inc., 2001); David O'Conner, *God and Inscrutable Evil* (New York: Rowman & Littlefield Publishers, 1998); Michael Peterson, *God and Evil* (Boulder, CO: Westview Press, 1998); Richard Swinburne, *Providence and the Problem of Evil* (Oxford: Clarendon Press, 1998); Daniel Howard-Snyder, ed., *The Evidential Argument from Evil* (Bloomington: Indiana University Press, 1996); Hans Schwarz, *Evil: A Historical and Theological Perspective,* trans. Mark Worthing (Minneapolis: Fortress Press, 1995); R. Douglas Geivett, *Evil and The Evidence for God* (Philadelphia: Temple University Press, 1993); Michael Peterson, *The Problem of Evil: Selected Readings* (Notre Dame: University of Notre Dame Press, 1992).
33. It is important to say at this juncture that I am not suggesting the theodicy offered in this book is necessarily convincing or comprehensive; rather, it is an attempt to shift the paradigm for a new approach to answering the argument from evil.
34. Peterson, *God and Evil*, 87.
35. Some may be satisfied with a position that simply confesses much of life as a mystery, but it is not a consistent position. The premise of biblical faith is that God has revealed Himself and His ways to mankind. The claim is not that we have exhaustive knowledge, but that we have sufficient knowledge. Thus, to take refuge in unexplainability is to presume that divine revelation is insufficient at a critical point in establishing the biblical worldview.
36. This too is possible but inconsistent with well-established doctrines such as the doctrine of creation itself. If God created the world, the world cannot be inconsistent with God's character. If time and space are created by God, then clearly they are not contrary to God as revealed in the Incarnation.
37. Peterson, *God and Evil*, 86.
38. Examples of this are found in: Millard Erickson, *God the Father Almighty* (Grand Rapids: Baker Book House, 1998); Michael Peterson, *God and Evil* (Boulder, CO: Westview Press, 1998); David Basinger, *The Case for Freewill Theism* (Downers Grove: InterVarsity Press, 1996); Clark Pinnock and others, *The Openness of God* (Downers Grove: InterVarsity Press, 1994).

39. Ibid., 88.
40. Ibid., 103.
41. The term 'evangelical' is used to identify the contemporary Christian theological position that emphasizes the importance of personal religious commitments and affirms the historic doctrines of orthodox Christianity. These include: the Trinitarian nature of God, the deity and virgin birth of Jesus Christ, salvation by grace alone through faith in the substitutionary death of Christ, His Resurrection, the personal return of Christ at the end of the age, and the infallibility of Scripture.
42. Lewis, *The Problem of Pain*, 33.
43. Ibid., 25.
44. This would be those who subscribe to the *openness* view of God, which claims that God does not know the future choices of His moral agents.

2

THE HISTORICAL CONTEXT
OF GREATER-GOOD THEODICIES

This chapter reviews three varieties of the G-G theodicy as developed by Augustine of Hippo, Thomas Aquinas, and Gottfried Leibniz. Each one affirms that God exists and develops some form of a greater-good explanation for why evil continues to exist in God's created order. The three share certain common ideas regarding the problem of evil, and, as R. Douglas Geivett concludes, even the theodicy of Leibniz shares in "the tradition established by his precursors Augustine and Aquinas."[1] One important common point is the belief that there are positive arguments for God's existence. As Geivett notes, each one agrees on the "important role of traditional arguments for the existence of God."[2] In fact, Aquinas developed his *Five Ways* in the context of considering the argument from evil. If evil is an argument against God's existence, he reasoned, then it is wise to determine if there is any evidence for God's existence. In keeping with this historic theological position, we will see that in each G-G theodicy to be considered, there is a general commitment to an understanding of God as the One who is omnipotent, omniscient and omni-benevolent.

I readily admit that the G-G theodicy does have a long history of acceptance among Christians. However, as I will maintain, in the end, the G-G theodicy fails at several levels. I think the G-G theodicy satisfied many when certain other beliefs were standard fare among the general population. Assumptions were not questioned, but it is not so today. We live in a different time: the questions have expanded and the core beliefs have decreased. I do not mean to suggest that there are no answers to the questions from evil, but only that the typical ones given have proven unsatisfactory. I firmly believe that regardless of how deficient past answers may have been; evil is not a defeater of belief in God's existence. The conclusion of the G-G theodicy is right; that is, God is morally justified in allowing evil in this world. What is addressed here is the argument itself, not the conclusion of the G-G theodicies.

AUGUSTINE

In attempting to absolve God of any culpability for evil in the world and to explain its presence in God's created order, Augustine of Hippo (A.D. 354–430) developed an explanation for the existence of evil based on the actuality of human free will. His defense recognized the actuality of human free will (as man was in the garden before the Fall), a tradition continued by both Aquinas and Leibniz. Augustine began his discussion with the conviction that God exists and that a right understanding of the issues of life and death must be predicated upon and interpreted by this truth. For Augustine, a right view of God required that:

> We believe Him [God] to be almighty, utterly unchangeable, the creator of all things that are good, though Himself more excellent than they, the utterly just ruler of all He has created, self-sufficient and therefore without any assistance from any other being in the act of creation. It follows from this that He created all out of nothing.[3]

Augustine then moved to the moral question of the problem of evil, which focused on the evidential version of the problem.

Concerning the source of evil, Augustine argued that the evil results from an inappropriate act of the human will. God had not given man's will for that purpose; however, it made wrong choices a possibility. Adam was created in grace, but that grace "did not include a confirmed perseverance in good, but the choice between good and evil was left to the decision of his free will."[4] The will was free "so they [Adam and Eve] may act for or against the divine will."[5] Unfortunately, man's will turned away from God—not because God determined it to be so, but because man chose the lesser good. The will was free to choose, which meant that God bore no responsibility for the resulting evil, as the will itself was good.

As Augustine explains, just "because sin occurs through free will, we must not suppose that God gave man free will for the purpose of sinning. It is a sufficient reason why it ought to be given, that man cannot live rightly without it."[6] Geivett points out that by "living rightly", Augustine means "leading a righteous life. Such a life is one that is morally praiseworthy or commendable."[7] Living for God was to be a choice, and it was God's intent that man should choose the good.

Louis Berkhof notes that Augustine taught that had man "proved obedient, he would have been confirmed in holiness. From the state of *posse non peccare et mori* (the ability not to sin and die) he would have passed to the state of the *non posse peccare et mori* (the inability to sin and die). But he sinned, and consequently entered the state of the *non posse non peccare et mori* (the inability not to sin and die)."[8] The act of the will to choose to disobey did not flow from some evil in the will itself; rather, it was the improper exercise of the will. The will could not be evil as it came from God, and whatever comes from God is good, for God alone is good. Free will, that which was necessary for man to be man, was one of those good things because it came from God.

According to Augustine, goods could be put into three categories. He writes:

> Virtues, then, by which we live rightly, are great goods, but all kinds of bodily beauty, without which we can live rightly, are the least goods. The powers of the soul, without which we cannot live rightly, are the middle goods. No one uses the virtues wrongly, but anyone can use the other goods, middle and the least, wrongly as well as rightly.[9]

The will belongs to the middle good and as such is good in and of itself, but has the power to turn to either the unchanging good or the changing good. The will, unfortunately, turned away from the unchanging good to the changing good. This "turning away" for Augustine anticipates, as Robert O'Connell points out, "(t)hat the consequences flow inexorably from the very nature of the soul's own evil act. Turn away 'perversely' from union with the Highest reality, and by its very nature the turn must be a turn toward lesser realities; it can have no other terminus except the 'diminishment' and 'privation' of being which Augustine equates with 'corruption,' evil."[10] God's grace, however, can overcome the influence of this vitiated will if man will look to this grace.

According to Augustine, it is not that God gave man good things and bad things from which to choose, but goods of different categories (*higher goods* and *lower goods*). Everything that man was given from which to choose could be classified as a *good*. God did not give man bad things from which to choose because all that was had been created by God. Whereas evil has no essence of its own, it cannot exist as an independent entity. Evil is in the will turning from the unchangeable good to the changeable good. Augustine writes:

> The will, then if it clings to the unchangeable good which is common to all, obtains the principal and important human goods, though the will itself is a middle good. But the will sins, if it turns away from the unchangeable good which is common to all, and turns towards private good, whether outside or below it. . . . Evil is the turning of the will away from the unchangeable good, and towards changeable good. Since this turning from one to the other is free and unforced, the pain which follows as a punishment is fitting and just.[11]

Arguing that the corruption came through a turning of the will in a wrong direction while affirming that the will was good required an explanation of the cause responsible for the will's turning wrongly. That is, why did or what caused the will to turn from the unchangeable to the changeable? Did the will move by its own power in that direction? If so, then of course, God would be responsible for sin, since He made the will with the inclination to turn from the unchangeable to the changeable. As Augustine notes regarding the will, if "the will which was given, of its very nature moves as it does, it cannot help turning in this direction. There cannot be any fault, if nature and necessity compel it."[12] Therefore, Augustine maintains that the will does not turn by necessity, but is culpable for its own turning. He notes:

So what need is there to ask the source of that movement by which the will turns from the unchangeable good to the changeable good? We agree that it belongs only to the soul, and is voluntary and therefore culpable; and the whole value of teaching in this matter consists in its power to make us censure and check this movement, and turn our wills away from temporal things below us to enjoyment of the everlasting good.[13]

The power of the will, Augustine argues, resides in the soul and could not come from a natural inclination of the will. The will comes from God and only good comes from God. Plainly, he argues that one cannot go further than this: "Perverted will, then, is the cause of all evil."[14] Free will is necessary for man to be man (a moral being). The only way man can do right is if he has the power of will to choose to do right. Man simply cannot *do* right without free will (*libertarian freedom*). It is necessary to human*ness*.

The truth is, Augustine argued, God's giving man free will must be considered as one of the crowning acts of the gracious and good God. This, he maintained, was a good act of God even though it led to terrible consequences for man when he misused his free will to choose the least of the goods. Yet, if God knew that the will of man would turn in the wrong direction, then there was the question of the relationship between God's knowledge of what happened and His causing what happened.

This is the question of whether or not God's foreknowledge caused man to sin. The argument is that if God foreknew that man would sin, and since God only knows all true things, man was determined to sin. This supposedly follows logically from the position that God cannot know any non-true state of affairs, so if He knows something will be, then it must be and cannot be otherwise. Augustine responds that this would not be the case. He reasons that if a person foreknew that another will sin; this does not mean that the foreknowledge causes the sin. Augustine concludes "Your foreknowledge would not be the cause of his sin, though undoubtedly he would sin; otherwise, you would not foreknow that this would happen. Therefore, these two are not contradictory—your foreknowledge and someone else's free act. So, too, God compels no one to sin, though He foresees those who will sin by their own will."[15]

God's knowledge of the fact that man would sin and that man in actuality did sin was not a causal relationship. Man's will, Augustine argues, operated independently of God's foreknowledge, but not outside the scope of His foreknowledge, thus avoiding the idea that God caused man's will to turn in the direction it did. As Robert Brown points out, Augustine holds to the "compatibility of human free will (on an indeterminist account) with divine omniscience."[16] Augustine denies that God's knowledge of man's turning away from Him was causal knowledge.

Gratuitous Evil

Augustine's application of his foundational view of God denies the possibility of gratuitous evil—all evil has a purpose because God is omni-benevolent and sovereign, assuring that all things have a divine purpose. He notes "In relation to the whole, to the ordered connection of all creation in space and time, no one whatever can be created without a purpose. Not even the leaf of a tree is created without a purpose."[17] God not only created all things for a purpose, but also because of His omni-benevolence and His providence, one can be assured that God will bring good from the evil He permits in His world as a result of the Fall. God will not allow evil to override His good purposes for His creation, even though man unwisely uses his will against God.

For Augustine, even the suffering of children has redemptive value, for "God does good in correcting adults when their children whom they love suffer pain and death."[18] If children suffer, however, no good accrues to them, at least not in Augustine's scheme. The good is that parents become better parents. But this leaves open the question of whether a better parent is a sufficient good in order to justify the horrible suffering of an innocent.

Augustine maintains that the all-powerful God can work in space and time, turning the evil that comes about by man's free will in order to bring about a greater good. In this theodicy, no evil is pointless (or gratuitous). If God can not bring good out of the evil, then in His providence, this evil state of affairs would not exist. Further, God can bring good out of any amount of evil, great or small. Clearly, God is not responsible for evil because it comes by man's misuse of something good (free will), and yet, in God's providence He brings good from the evil.

Summary

Augustine began his discussion with the conviction that God was all-good and all-powerful and then asked the question: "I should like you to tell me: is God the cause of evil?"[19] He did not argue that evil was the necessary path by which God did something better in creation. Evil resulted from the turning of the will, which was good in and of itself. Because God is good, He ultimately turns all evil for good, for all things in God's providence have a purpose. Evil is a privation. It is not something in and of itself. It is a lack. Augustine understood evil, not as something that was a created substance, but a lack in the good substance as created by God.

Augustine's discussion of evil turns not on what he gathers from the evidence, but rather from his theological understanding and application of the goodness and providence of God. For Augustine, the good is free will (*libertarian freedom*); that is, man is greater because he has the freedom of the will, and when the will turns wrongly, God brings a greater good from the resulting evil. Therefore, there is the greater-good on two counts for Augustine.

THOMAS AQUINAS

Thomas Aquinas (1225–1274) addresses the subject of evil in connection with his proofs for God's existence. He argues, as does Augustine, that a discussion about evil can only be understood correctly if viewed in light of the evidence that God does exist—a fact Aquinas argues could be "demonstrated from those of His effects which are known to us."[20] That is, although evil apparently argues against the all-powerful, all-good God's existence, other evidence in the world provides evidence to the contrary. Therefore, it is proper to begin with the evidence for God before considering the evidence against God. Even so, Aquinas confesses that the existence of evil makes it seem as though "God does not exist."[21] Therefore, although the evidence for the existence of God is compelling, Aquinas still thinks it necessary to respond to those who argue from the presence of evil to the non-existence of God.

Aquinas builds on the Augustinian notion of God's omnipotence and goodness and concludes that God will only allow evil if He can bring good from it. According to Aquinas, God in His providence and goodness will—and because of His nature must—bring good out of the evil; otherwise, He cannot permit the evil. Therefore, all evil leads to some good in the end because God has so ordained it. As with Augustine, Aquinas argues deductively, beginning with his theology proper. The good God brings out of evil is good in the general sense. Geisler suggests that Aquinas teaches that "not every specific event in the world has a good purpose; only the general purpose is good."[22] In the end, God's power prevails and good overcomes evil. That is, the good is restored.

The Cause of Evil

The question remains that if every being (God's creation) is good, then from where does evil come? Whereas God (the all-good One) cannot create evil substantively (essentially), how is evil related to God? Aquinas maintains that "evil has no formal cause; rather it is a privation of form; likewise, neither has it a final cause, but rather it is a privation of order to the proper end; since not only the end has the nature of good, but also the useful, which is ordered to the end. Evil, however, has a cause by way of an agent, not directly, but accidentally."[23] Aquinas makes it clear that God did not create evil. The cause of evil is "in the action otherwise than in the effect."[24] That is, man is not substantively evil (he is a creation of God). As Brian Davies writes, for Aquinas to say that "something is bad (or evil) is to say, not that it *has* something, but that it *lacks* something." This means that evil could not have been a part of God's initial creation as creation flowed from the mind of God and God's mind lacks nothing.

Both Augustine and Aquinas understand that free will itself did not necessitate evil, but only made evil possible. Aquinas points out that "Nevertheless the movement itself of an evil will is caused by the rational creature, which is good; and thus good is the cause of evil."[25] Aquinas makes it clear that his suggestion that good is the cause of evil should not be construed as his saying that God is the cause of evil. His point is that whereas evil is the privation of the good, if there was no good, there could be no evil. Aquinas, as Augustine, argues that evil results from some free negative act (the turning from the unchangeable good to the changeable good) of human will. Thus, God was not the direct cause of evil. As Davies argues, Aquinas holds that "God does not creatively will evil. All he wills is good. And he can only be said to will evil in the sense of permitting it, not in the sense of causing it directly."[26] God intended good things for man, not evil. Therefore, according to Aquinas, it is the defect within man (this wrong use of the will) that finds him at odds with his own purposes in finding this blessedness. Aquinas suggests, however, that some good will come from the evil God allows, and in part, this good involves some form of soul-making good.

Summary

In the end, there is no actual gratuitous evil in Aquinas's theodicy. In fact, all evil that God allows accomplishes something in the sufferer which could not have been achieved otherwise—if not in time, surely in eternity. This conclusion not only raises questions about gratuitous evil but about the greater-good notion in general. As Middleton points out, "Whereas the motivation of the greater good defense is admirable in that it attempts to retain an orthodox doctrine of God as both good and providentially sovereign in the face of evident evil, it is the strategy that is problematic."[27] It is built on an assumption of inference, namely, that an omnipotent and all-good God can not allow anything in His creation that does not serve a good purpose. This is seen in Augustine and now in Aquinas. It is, however, this very assumption that seems to open the greater-good approach to challenge, even from a classical theistic position.

GOTTFRIED VON LEIBNIZ

Gottfried Wilhelm Von Leibniz (1646–1716) in his treatise entitled *Theodicee (1710)* forwards the notion that this is the best of all possible worlds in spite of the fact at this particular time and place there is a lot of evil. Leibniz reasons that though one should fill all times and all places, it remains true that "one might have filled them in innumerable ways, and that there is an infinitude of possible worlds among which God must needs have chosen the best, since he does nothing without acting in accordance with supreme reason."[28] Many people have heard of Augustine and Aquinas, but Leibniz is not so familiar (unless you have read Voltaire). Nonetheless, Leibniz was an influential theologian of his day. Augustine, Aquinas, and Leibniz all believe that God is all-powerful and all-good, and can only create good. Only Leibniz, however, takes this view of God to its logical conclusion. For him, the fact that God is good necessarily means that what God has created is not only good ontologically; it was the best of all the possible worlds. Whereas all three argue deductively in some way beginning with God, Leibniz starts with God's character and what His character means for creation. For Leibniz, this means that this is the best of all possible worlds (or some might say, feasible worlds). I believe that this idea is the best of all possible worlds as maintained by Leibniz and is important for answering the question from evil.

The Best of All Possible Worlds

Leibniz maintains that the world God actualized was the best of all worlds that God knew, in his omniscience, could exist. This was true for every aspect of the world actualized, including man's *libertarian freedom*. Leibniz notes:

> Since, moreover, God's decrees consist solely in the resolution he forms, after having compared all possible worlds, to choose that one which is the best, and brought it into existence together with all that this world contains, by means of the all-powerful word *Fait*, it is plain to see that this decree changes nothing in the constitution of things: God leaves them just as they were in the state of mere possibility, that is, changing nothing either in their essence or nature, or even in their accidents, which are represented perfectly already in the idea of this possible world. Thus that which is contingent and free remains no less so under the decrees of God than under his prevision.[29]

Leibniz argues that God in His omniscience (middle knowledge) saw all the possible worlds and actualized the best of those worlds. Each of the worlds was, in part, shaped by the free choices of man. When He did this, He changed nothing in the actualizing of the world that was known in its state of possibility or potentiality. Of all the possible worlds God could have actualized, this is the world that God chose and it is the best of possible worlds. God, as the all-perfect and all-knowing being, could only do His best, which in this case was to bring into being (actualized existence) the best (not *perfect* in the same sense God is perfect) of the possible worlds.

Leibniz is careful not to make the idea of a best world a necessity as this would then open his position to the claim that God is not free; that is, God Himself is determined if He must of necessity create this world. He writes:

> There is always a prevailing reason which prompts the will to its choice, and for the maintenance of freedom for the will it suffices that this reason should incline without necessitating. That is also the opinion of all the ancients, of Plato, of Aristotle, of St. Augustine. The will is never prompted to action save by the representation of the good, which prevails over the opposite representations. This is admitted even in relation to God, the good angels, and souls in bliss: and it is acknowledged that they are none the less free in consequence of that. God fails not to choose the best, but he is not constrained to do so: nay, more, there is no necessity in the object of God's choice, for another sequence of things is equally possible. For that very reason the choice is free and independent of necessity, because it is made between several possibilities, and the will is determined only by the preponderating goodness of the object.[30]

God is totally free to create or not create. Once He chooses to create, it is morally impossible for God to create anything but the best of all possible worlds.

When Leibniz affirms that this is the best of all possible worlds, he is using the word *world* to identify all of created order, from start to finish. He explains, "I call 'World' the whole succession and the whole agglomeration of all existent things, lest it be said that several worlds could have existed in different times and different places. For they must needs be reckoned all together as one world, or if you will, as one Universe."[31] That is, "It is a continued creation."[32]

This flows from his idea that there were many possible worlds, but out of all the possible worlds that could be, God chose the best, and this world as a whole formed one book of that world. If there were to be a better world in the future, then God had not selected the best in His initial creation. As Peterson observes, for Leibniz, the best possible world "is a total possible state of affairs, a complete universe with past, present, and future."[33] As Leibniz makes clear, "Now this supreme wisdom, united to a goodness that is no less infinite, cannot but have chosen the best. For as a lesser evil is a kind of good, even so a lesser good is a kind of evil if it stands in the way of a greater good; and there would be something to correct in the actions of God if it were possible to do better."[34]

The Source of Evil

Like Augustine and Aquinas before him, Leibniz understands the central issue in the problem of evil to be the matter of man's free will. The will has its own power as one does not will to will (no infinite regress of the willing). Reason inclines it, but does not determine it. Leibniz writes "As for *volition* itself, to say that it is an object of free will is incorrect. We will to act, strictly speaking, and we do not will to will; else we could still say that we will to have the will to will, and that would go on to infinity."[35] This will, however, is not always guided by good judgment. Leibniz continues:

> Besides, we do not always follow the latest judgement of practical understand-
> ing when we resolve to will; but we always follow, in our willing, the result of
> all the inclinations that come from the direction both of reasons and passions,
> and this often happens without an express judgement of the understanding.[36]

Because the will depends on reason, it should follow that if man always judges rightly, he will act rightly.

Leibniz acknowledges that if one claims that free will has led to suffering, one must explain why the will turned in that direction. It could not be in the will, Leibniz reasons, because God made the will and all that God does is good. Therefore, he concludes that the answer must be found in that which is independent of man's will. This leads him to argue that the weakness is in the ideal nature of man. He writes "We must consider that there is an *original imperfection in the creature* before sin, because the creature is limited in his essence; whence ensues that it cannot know all, and that it can deceive itself and commit other errors."[37]

The nature of man, although it is good, is limited by the fact it was created (finite), which means man is finite in every respect, including knowledge. Therefore, it is impossible for man, as a creature, to know everything. The limitedness (man as a finite creature, which is not a moral imperfection) of man's ideal nature (his nature was good because it came from God) proved to be the cause of evil. Geivett says "Evil, in Leibniz's view, is a privative reality. It is an imperfection that comes from limitation."[38]

God is not responsible for the limitation, for all created beings, of necessity, have this limitation, as anything created cannot be limitless in all or any respects, for such an attribute belongs only to God who is uncreated. As Ed Miller points out, Leibniz teaches "(i)t would in fact be *logically impossible* to have a world without evil: Anything created by God would have to be *less* than God just by virtue of being *dependent* on him, and this means immediately that it must be less than perfect, and *this* means immediately the presence of various sorts of imperfections. How could God create something that was perfect, and therefore independent, and therefore uncreated? *It is logically* impossible."[39] This limitation is not a moral imperfection, but moral imperfection came from this limitedness. As Geivett explains Leibniz, evil "is an imperfection that comes from limitation."[40] This limitation is not evil. As a created entity it could not be perfect in the sense that God (a necessary being) is perfect.

Free Will

Free will entailing judgment places man above the rest of creation. Choices alone do not make for true freedom of choice. Rather, the ability to make a judgment (moral) about the choices must be added to choices. For Leibniz, free will also meant that the will has its own power. There is not a will that causes the will. Leibniz maintains that the will is free. Man's will, in order to be truly free, must be totally free:

> I am of the opinion that our will is exempt not only from constraint but also from necessity. Aristotle has already observed that there are two things in freedom, to wit, spontaneity and choice, and therein lies our mastery over our actions. . . . There is *contingency* in a thousand actions of Nature; but where there is no judgement in him who acts there is no *freedom*.[41]

The will is free to will as that is the purpose of the will, and the predetermination of God's decrees do not confound (though it may limit) this freedom. For Leibniz, God does decree, but there is no insult to the freedom He has chosen to give man, since free will is part of the best possible world. In fact, the notions of *best* and *possible* worlds are connected by the idea of free will. Since the best was a world where man had free will, that limited the possibilities of how that world would look, hence the best *possible* world.

Leibniz recognizes that to claim that this is the best of all possible worlds seems somewhat naive in light of the existing evil. Leibniz argues, however, that some would suggest that the best world would be one where no evil or sin exists. He simply replies "But I deny that then it would have been *better*."[42] His reasoning is that the world is a whole; to change one piece would be to change the whole. It appears that Leibniz has made an important point concerning the connectedness within this world and that it is correct to assert that changing the world in one place will have implications for the whole.

He further points out that the case for the presence of evil in this world can be made from an evidential perspective as well. It is "a little evil that renders the good more discernable, that is to say, greater."[43] Having said this, Leibniz realized there was more than a little evil in the world. Hereby, he responds to the one who argues that there is no reason evil should outnumber good by so much. He postulates a greater good in that "if we were unusually sick and seldom in good health, we should be wonderfully sensible of that great good and we should be less sensible of our evils."[44] Leibniz holds to the position that although God is not properly responsible for evil, He does in fact permit it, and brings a greater good from it.

In the end, God, by duty to Himself, must always antecedently will what is good, for He is good and wills consequently the best from all acts, including evil. Evil only exists because God was being true to Himself by doing His best when creating this world. The best of all possible worlds is not necessarily one without evil, but the amount of evil is commensurate with this being, on the whole, the best world. In fact, Leibniz does not argue that this is a perfect world, only the best world.

CONCLUSION

Augustine, Aquinas, and Leibniz agree that evil has resulted through the reality of man's free will. The will is not sinful itself, but it exercises itself in such a way as to choose against, instead of for, God. All three, while differing in some of the details, agree that God is able to bring good out of evil. In fact, God uses evil to obtain a greater good. All three argued (not necessarily on the same grounds) that gratuitous evil does not exist. Unique to Leibniz, however, is his idea that this is the best of all possible worlds.

Leibniz's point that this is the best of all possible worlds flows naturally from his emphasis on the fact that God is all-perfect. Though God is all-perfect, the world that exists by creation cannot be God, and therefore the world cannot be perfect as God is. Therefore, if there *were* to be a world, certain necessary conditions dictate what would make that world possible. Since Augustine and Aquinas (and others) agree that a world with creatures with free will in it is better than one without such, Leibniz is within the Augustinian tradition in arguing that *best* would at least have to entail man having free will. Given that, if it is really to be free will (understood as *libertarian freedom*), Leibniz argues, there would be a number of directions in which things could go (i.e. there were many possible worlds). God, seeing all the possibilities (due to His omniscience) chose this world (demonstrating His omnipotence), which under the order of free will (which is a necessary part of being a good world), would be the best (God being all-perfect). In this world, man would act freely, but it was this exact world that God determined with all the choices (good and bad), prayers, and other realities. That is, there were other possible choices, but they were not a part of this world; therefore, man did not get the opportunity to make those choices. By God's choosing out of all the possible worlds, God determined which world mankind would live in.

When Leibniz is compared with both Augustine and Aquinas in the matter of gratuitous evil all three claim that gratuitous evil does not exist. Leibniz, however, arrives at his position differently. Leibniz argues that this is the best of all possible worlds based on the fact that God is the all-perfect one. Therefore, He chooses the world where the evil brings about some good. So, Leibniz's position flows from the fact that God is all-perfect. Augustine and Aquinas argue for no gratuitous evil based on the fact of God's omnipotence and goodness. They (and many others who have followed) assume that if God is all-powerful and all-good, then He cannot permit gratuitous evil in His created order. The question is whether this position can be the correct position given the apparent existence of *gratuitous evil*; i.e., evil that seemingly does not result in a greater good or even any good at all.

NOTES

1. R. Douglas Geivett, *Evil and The Evidence for God* (Philadelphia: Temple University Press, 1993), 27.
2. Ibid., 28.
3. St. Augustine, *The Problem of Free Choice*. trans. Dom Mark Pontifix in *Ancient Christian Writers*, ed. Johannes Quasten & Joseph Plumpe (Westminster, Maryland: The Newman Press, 1955), 1.1.1. All quotes are cited from this source.
4. Jaroslav Pelikan, *The Christian Tradition*, vol. 1, *The Emergence of the Catholic Tradition (100-600)* (Chicago: University of Chicago Press, 1975), 299.
5. Vernon J. Bourke, *Augustine's Love of Wisdom* (West Lafayette, IN: Purdue University Press, 1992), 33.
6. Augustine, *The Problem of Free Choice*, 2.1.3.
7. Geivett, *Evil and the Evidence for God*, 15.
8. Louis Berkhof, *The History of Christian Doctrines* (Grand Rapids: Baker Book House, 1975), 134.
9. Ibid., 2.19.50.
10. Robert J. O'Connell, S.J., *Images of Conversion in St. Augustine's Confessions* (New York: Fordham University Press, 1996), 181.
11. Augustine, *The Problem of Free Choice*, 2.19.53.
12. Augustine, *The Problem of Free Choice*, 2.1.1.
13. Ibid., 3.1.2.
14. Ibid., 3.17.48.
15. Ibid., 3.4.10.
16. Robert F. Brown, "Divine Omniscience, Immutability, Aseity and Human Free Will," *Religious Studies* 27 (1991): 286.
17. Augustine, *The Problem of Free Choice*, 3.23.66.
18. Augustine, *The Problem of Free Choice*, 3.23.68.

19. Ibid., 1.1.1.
20. Thomas Aquinas, *Summa Theologiae* 1.2.2. All quotes are cited from Volume One, Part One of the English Dominican Translation of Aquinas (1911) unless otherwise indicated [CD-ROM] (Albany, OR: Ages Software, 1998).
21. Ibid., 1.2.3.
22. Norman Geisler, *Thomas Aquinas: An Evangelical Appraisal* (Grand Rapids: Baker Book House, 1991), 159.
23. Aquinas, *Summa Theologiae,* 1.49.1.
24. Ibid., 1.49.1.
25. Ibid., 1.49.1.1.
26. Brian Davies, *The Thought of Thomas Aquinas* (Oxford: Clarendon Press, 1992), 96–7.
27. Richard J. Middleton, "Why the 'Greater-Good' Isn't a Defense," 9 *Koinonia* (1997), 90.
28. G. W. Leibniz, *Theodicy,* ed. by Austin Farrer and trans. by E. M. Huggard (LaSalle, IL: Open Court, 1951), 128. This edition will be the text cited below.
29. Ibid., 151.
30. Ibid., 148.
31. Ibid., 128.
32. Ibid., 139.
33. Michael L. Peterson, *God and Evil: An Introduction to the Issues* (Boulder, CO: Westview Press, 1998), 92.
34. Ibid.
35. Leibniz, *Theodicy,* 151.
36. Ibid.
37. Ibid., 135.
38. Geivett, *Evil and the Evidence for God,* 26.
39. Ed L. Miller, *Questions that Matter,* 3rd ed. (New York: McGraw-Hill, 1992), 356.
40. Geivett, *Evil and the Evidence for God,* 26.
41. Leibniz, *Theodicy,* 143.
42. Ibid., 128.
43. Ibid., 130.
44. Ibid.

3

REVIEW OF CONTEMPORARY THEODICIES

In the last chapter I gave a brief overview regarding how the Church has formed an answer to the question about evil in the world. That took us up to the seventeenth century. Now I would like to present a sampling of contemporary responses to the question from evil. For that, I will review the theodicies of John Hick, Richard Swinburne and Michael Peterson. These three have been selected for review because of their recognized work in the area of theodicy. In each case we will see that they endorse some variety of the greater-good scheme. I would say that although in the end I will disagree with each one's basic approach; nonetheless, each has contributed something to the ongoing work of theodicy, particularly in answering the atheist's evidential argument from evil.

I think it is important for us to see how different theodicies that appropriate the idea of the greater good work out as a whole. That is, it is important to see where this idea of the greater good as the moral justification for God allowing evil leads. Therefore, the following reviews are intended to illustrate how G-G theodicies explain certain important issues relative to evil. Each review contains a brief critique on major points. Several issues will receive particular attention: gratuitous evil, free will, libertarian freedom, God's omniscience, the state of man in the afterlife, and whether or not this is the best of all possible worlds. Other G-G theodicies might well have been included; however, these three seem to be a good representation of contemporary attempts at theodicy.

JOHN HICK

Hick begins his theodicy by affirming the traditional view of God as the all-good and all-powerful God. In addition, he accepts the Irenaean view of Adam as created in need of being perfected. In this view "man, the finite, personal creature capable of personal relationship with his Maker is as yet only potentially the perfected being whom God is seeking to produce."[1] He believes this is the most promising starting point for theodicy. Hick urges "Let us now try to formu-

mature creature beginning the long process of further growth and development."[2] Consequently, for Hick, soul-making is God's intention for man and it is only accomplished through suffering in this life. Through suffering the soul is perfected, and the perfected soul is the greater good that comes from human suffering.

The Fall

Whereas man was not created in a spiritually mature state, Hick argues that man must grow into the perfected state. Therefore, Hick, in the tradition of Irenaeus, suggests that man's spiritual maturing involves a two-stage process. At least in principle[3], he follows Irenaeus' notion that there is a difference between "the image of God" and the "likeness of God", which forms Hick's two-stage maturing process for man. He explains it as the process where individual persons are led from "human *Bios*, or the biological life of man, to the quality of *Zoe*, or the personal life of eternal worth which we see in Christ. . . ."[4] Through the struggle within a hostile environment over the last four thousand years or so, "[U]ncounted millions of souls have been through the experience of earthly life, and God's purpose has gradually moved towards its fulfillment within each one of them, . . ."[5] According to Hick, man is made by divine power in the "image of God", but only through the struggle encountered in the hostile environment in which man lives is it possible to achieve the second intention of God, namely man developing into the "likeness of God."

The first stage, which came about by divine power, includes "the development of man as a rational and responsible person capable of personal relationship with the personal Infinite who created him."[6] This stage is what Hick identifies by the phrase "image of God" and makes much of the idea that the finite is designed to have a personal relationship with the infinite One, a point I think of great significance. Whereas for Hick the "personal life is essentially free and self-directing,"[7] it is not possible that it should be subjected to the controlling or determining power of God. This is another very important point, namely that this relationship between man and God was to be one of mutual love; man must be free to enter into that relationship or it would not be a relationship of love.

The second stage is signaled by the term "likeness", which points to "the certain valuable quality of life which reflects finitely the divine life"[8] and cannot be accomplished by God's omnipotence. This second stage is what Hick refers to as the *soul-making stage*. The value of life in this world is not determined primarily by either the pain or pleasure it brings but "by its fitness for its primary purpose, the purpose of soul-making."[9] For the soul-making process to move forward, man must be placed in an environment where temptation and struggle exist as a means to the soul-making end. As Hick writes, "The value-judgement that is implicitly being invoked here is that one who has attained to goodness by meeting and eventually mastering temptations, and thus by rightly making responsible choices in concrete situations, is a good in a richer and more valuable sense than would be one created *ab initio* in a state either of innocence or virtue."[10] As Marilyn M. Adams points out, Hick sees God's soul-making project culminating "in a process of spiritual development in which autonomous created persons, with their own free participation, are perfected, fashioned into God's likeness, formed towards the pattern of Christ."[11] Hick's starting point has evil as a necessary part of God's plan in order to perfect man, a position that raises, what I would suggest, some serious theological questions.

Libertarian Freedom

Hick argues that the perfecting process becomes a reality by the exercise of man's free choice in learning what is the good (or right) as he faces temptation, struggles, and risks. It is not his free choice that is matured, but only through the exercise of his free choice is he perfected spiritually. I think Hick's greatest contribution comes when he notes that it "is not only that they shall freely act rightly towards one another but that they shall also freely enter into a filial personal relationship with God Himself."[12] It would be logically impossible, Hick concludes, for God to manipulate nature and environment so that man would choose to love Him, although it might be logically possible for God to make free man always to do right. If God made man so that he would necessarily love God, then man's actions would not be the result of the free exercise of his choice. This would seriously erode the idea of both free will and love as traditionally understood. Furthermore, Hick maintains that if God manipulates man so that man can only love God, there would be something "inauthentic about the resulting trust, love, or service."[13] Authentic love and worship require the freedom to choose that path.

If man is really free to love God, Hick claims that there must be an actual distance between the infinite and the finite so that man will sense no pressure to love God. He writes "In creating finite persons to love and be loved by Him God must endow them with a certain relative autonomy over against Himself. But how can a finite creature, dependent upon the infinite Creator for its very existence and for every power and quality of its being, possess any significant autonomy in relation to that Creator?"[14] In other words, there must be some "epistemic distance"[15] between the Infinite One and the finite ones if there is to be any true sense of freedom on the part of the created ones.

According to Hick, epistemic distance means that "the reality and presence of God must not be borne in upon men in the coercive way in which their natural environment forces itself upon their attention."[16] Epistemic distance is God setting man at a distance from himself so that man's freedom to choose to love God would be totally free—no subtle undue influence from God. This distance is not total distance, however, as it has been constructed in such a way that man can have some knowledge of God, but "only in a mode of knowledge that involves a free personal response on man's part, this response consisting in an uncompelled interpretative activity whereby we experience the world as mediating the divine presence."[17]

This, he suggests, means that in a sense the world must not have some overpowering influence upon men whereby they would have no option but to acknowledge and love God. This is not to say that one cannot see God in the universe, but only that the acknowledgment must be of such a nature that it permits a true freedom of choice, where man is free either to acknowledge or to ignore God. Whatever is visible of God in the universe, it must in no way bear unnecessary influence upon man in such a way that he would have no choice but to love God. Such conditions are necessary according to Hick if man is to be truly free in his experience to choose to love God. Only under this state of affairs can man be said to be a free moral being who can enter into an authentic filial relationship with God. I think Hick makes an excellent point regarding what is required if man is to have an authentic love for God.

The Greater Good Obtains

Hick maintains that in the end the good obtains, which as you will remember is that the soul-making in each individual will be accomplished. However, when dealing with the horrific evils, he appears to equivocate. In one place Hick argues that when bad things happen man may simply miss the good that comes from it. He says, "It is true that sometimes—no one can know how often or how seldom—there are sown or there comes to flower even in the direst calamity graces of character that seem to make even the calamity itself worthwhile."[18] But then he confesses that the contrary could be true:

> It may also fail to happen, and instead of gain there may be sheer loss. Instead of ennobling, affliction may crush the character and wrest from it whatever virtues it possessed. Can anything be said, from the point of view of Christian theodicy, in the face of this cosmic handling of man, which seems at best to be utterly indifferent and at worst implacably malevolent towards him?[19]

For example, when addressing the question of the Nazi crimes against the Jews, Hick maintains, "It would have been better—much much better—if they had never happened. Most certainly God did not want those who committed these fearful crimes against humanity to act as they did. His purpose for the world was retarded by them and the power of evil within it increased."[20]

Here, it appears that Hick is willing to admit that evil sometimes works counter to the purposes of God, in which case the claim that the good always obtains does not always hold true. If the good does not obtain, then gratuitous evil would be a reality, which is something Hick denies. As with most people who honestly deal with evil, what often defeats a theodicy is the reality of horrific evils. We must remember that horrific evils can be in terms both in extent (the Holocaust) and in kind (the rape and murder of the nine-year old).

Hans Schwarz charges that Hick can give "no answer as to the why of the Nazi crimes,"[21] which indicates Hick's theodicy stumbles at a most important point—horrific evil. When pressed for consistency Hick refuses to give in and simply confesses that his only response is a "frank appeal to the positive value of mystery."[22] Hick is sure that the greater good is obtained as a God of love would permit no other, so it is a mystery.

Here I would like to point out something about the appeal to mystery as so many Christians do this. I do affirm that there are mysteries when it comes to understanding the ways of God. However, I think it is theologically questionable to appeal to mystery in order to ignore blatant contradictions in our theological systems. I say this because one test for truth is internal consistency; that is, different parts of our theological systems must cohere, and if they do not, it is reason to believe at some point our system has gone awry. Hick, as so many others, only argues that "It would be an intolerable thought that God had permitted the fearful evil of sin without having already intended to bring out of it an even greater good than would have been possible if evil had never existed."[23]

Hick's explanation seems only to raise more questions. Hick's explanation makes evil necessary to the plan of God as it enables God to do something He could not have otherwise done. Yet, Hick also protests that he is not claiming that "each evil which occurs is specifically necessary to the attainment of the eventual end-state of perfected humanity in the divine Kingdom."[24] If this is so, does this mean that some evil does not accomplish its purpose—that is to say, it is pointless? I think it is easy to see that at this point Hick's theodicy begins to break down.

In the end, Hick admits that while concrete answers may be difficult, nonetheless, gratuitous evil does not exist. He writes "Moreover, I do not now have an alternative theory to offer that would explain in any rational way or ethical way why men suffer as they do. The only appeal left is to mystery."[25] He argues that "there could not be a person-making world devoid of what we call evil; and evils are never tolerable—except for the sake of greater goods which may come out of them."[26] Hick is bothered neither by the circuity of his argument nor by the contradiction of his position.

Universalism

Hick admits that suffering does not always complete its task in this life. His conclusion is:

> This world, with all its unjust and apparently wasted suffering, may nevertheless be what the Irenaean strand of Christian thought affirms that it is, namely a divinely created sphere of soul-making. But if this is so, yet further difficult questions now arise. A vale of soul-making that successfully makes persons of the desired quality may perhaps be justified by this result. But if the soul-making purpose fails, there can surely be no justification for 'the heavy and the weary weight of all this unintelligible world'. And yet, so far as we can see, the soul-making process does in fact fail in our own world at least as often as it succeeds.[27]

If soul-making is not accomplished in this life, then at some point after death some suffering will accomplish the perfection of the soul. As Hick suggests, this causes us to rethink the doctrine of hell. He concludes that the "needs of Christian theodicy compel us to repudiate the idea of eternal punishment."[28] For Hick, the only way the good purposes of a loving God can be met in suffering is if all men are saved (made perfect). Now we can see that Hick is trying to be consistent with his position. He concludes that God must accomplish the soul's perfection after the death.

Souls not won to God in time through suffering will be brought to God after death through suffering "within some further environment in which God places us."[29] Hick admits that this is an idea not "far from the traditional Roman Catholic notion of purgatorial experiences"[30] by which the soul ultimately reaches moral perfection. This, however, is not exactly what Hick has in mind. He does acknowledge that if the suffering in time fails to accomplish the soul-making process, then it can only be that the soul will be perfected after death, for if one soul fails, then the God of love has failed. The idea is that God in love has allowed the evil to perfect the soul, so all souls must be perfected either in this life or in the life to come.

According to Hick, this may happen in what he calls "a series of lives, each bounded by something analogous to birth and death, lived in other worlds in spaces other than that in which we now are."[31] Hick explains his view of man reaching his spiritual perfection in the afterlife by positing a middle ground between purgatory and reincarnation. S. Davis asserts that Hick's posture with universal salvation argues that "in the afterlife God will continue to respect our freedom; no one will be forced into the Kingdom, so to speak. But God has an infinite amount of time to work with and an infinite number of arguments to use."[32] It seems that Hick has gone to rather extravagant lengths to salvage his theodicy.

Summary

In the end, Hick's theodicy not only has theological assumptions that tend to weaken its appeal to the classical theist, but it also appears to have several inconsistencies as a system. Moreover, his universalism does not rescue his theodicy from its soul-making weaknesses. Aside from the theological issues, his failure to explain what appears to be gratuitous evil raises serious questions.

This has led Kane to conclude that Hick's theodicy is "either self-defeating or is merely a speculative conceptual scheme having no demonstrated capacity to explain the evils that actually exist in our world."[33] In the words of Schwarz, "Hick is unable to offer a plausible theodicy."[34] Geivett expresses his theological concerns over Hick's theodicy because Hick is "so willing to give up universally acknowledged conditions of orthodoxy within the Christian tradition."[35] In addition, one might also point out that his theodicy appears weightless in the issue of natural evils. As Barry Whitney writes "The problem of explaining why God allows physical evil is, perhaps, an even more difficult question than the problem of moral evil." Whitney also mentions that "a number of serious critical questions have been levied against Hick's theodicy at this point."[36] He admits that Hick attempts to answer these questions in his second edition of *Evil and the God of Love*, but having examined this edition, one is still hard-pressed to find consistent answers to these questions. It is hard to see how some natural evils contribute to the soul-making notion in Hick's theodicy.

While these are serious weaknesses in Hick's theodicy, I think the one positive aspect of his theodicy is his discussion of the importance of human freedom as a necessary ability of man that man might love God. I believe this is a very important contribution to the discussion of evil. So while I think Hick's theodicy is unacceptable for reasons given, his contribution is in arguing for the necessity of libertarian freedom.

RICHARD SWINBURNE

Richard Swinburne offers a theodicy because, in his estimation, "[w]ithout a theodicy, evil counts against the existence of God."[37] He thinks the "Christian doctrine of Providence is itself a central Christian doctrine," which can be defended against objections "when given its specifically Christian form."[38] Furthermore, Swinburne's understanding of the traditional task of theodicy[39] is not necessarily to give "an account of God's actual reasons for allowing a bad state to occur, but an account of his possible reasons (i.e., reasons which God has for allowing the bad state to occur, whether or not those are the ones which motivate him)."[40] He believes that God's good purposes are or "will be realized in the world"[41] and that the "good states which (according to Christian doctrine) God seeks are so good that they outweigh the accompanying evil."[42] In fact, Swinburne thinks that the good from suffering involves the development of one's character.

Libertarian Freedom

At the center of Swinburne's theodicy is the concept of free will, which for him is the libertarian understanding of freedom.[43] Concerning libertarian freedom, Swinburne points out that "the Christian theological tradition is that all Christian theologians of the first four centuries believed in human free will in the libertarian sense, as did all subsequent Eastern Orthodox theologians, and most Western Catholic theologians from Duns Scotus (in the fourteenth century) onwards."[44] By "libertarian freedom", Swinburne means that the agent's intentional action is not fully caused by either some process of natural causation (i.e., in virtue of laws of nature) or in some other way (e.g., by an agent such as God acting from outside the natural order).[45] He is convinced that the free will defense "becomes more plausible only if 'free will' means libertarian free will."[46] I think Swinburne makes a very good point in this declaration.

According to Swinburne, if the only view of free will is that of the compatibilist,[47] then God is ultimately the cause of evil unless "it can be shown that any actual bad choice is a necessary condition of some good state of affairs. . . ."[48] He suggests the compatibilist position makes the task of theodicy very difficult as it requires showing that "allowing the bad to occur is *logically* necessary for the attainment of good."[49] Swinburne thinks demonstrating this to be the case is a most difficult and unnecessary task for the theist.

For Swinburne, the greater good lies in the free will of man even though man may choose wrong. If evil results from man's free will (and it has), evil in God's universe is morally justified on the grounds that the greater good is man having free will. Swinburne maintains that it is, in fact, this libertarian freedom that stands at the center of understanding evil, both in terms of Adam's sin and all who follow.

God's Omniscience

Swinburne argues that "[O]n the assumption that God's knowledge of the future is limited by the libertarian free will which he [God] gives to humans, even God cannot know in advance for certain the actual amount of harm one individual will suffer at the hands of another in a given situation."[50] Swinburne believes that God is omniscient with qualification: "An omniscient being is one who knows everything logically possible for him to know, anything the description of his knowing which does not involve a contradiction."[51] However, "He will not necessarily know everything that will happen unless it is already predetermined that it will happen."[52] What God can know (at least) is all past and present events as well as all future events He has determined. What He cannot know is the future choices of His moral agents. As Jerry Walls observes, "According to Swinburne, God knows everything that is possible to know, but the future actions of free persons are not knowable in principle. So not even God can know with certainty what actions free persons will perform."[53]

Swinburne thinks that God can "predict human behavior correctly most of the time, but always with the possibility that men may falsify those predictions."[54] Further, he argues that suggesting God foreknows all the possible worlds He can create, all the free beings, and under what circumstances each would choose to do good or bad unnecessarily complicates and frustrates the theist's work of theodicy. In the end, Swinburne holds to an "openness" view of God's knowledge, which means God does not know the future choices of His moral beings. The matter of the "openness of God" has received considerable attention from the evangelical world recently, and if this view is necessary to Swinburne's theodicy, then I think it is safe to say it would make his theodicy rather unattractive to evangelicals. Certainly I would see this as a major challenge to his theodicy.

Greater Good

For Swinburne, the greater good is found in the reality of man's free will, but also in the general order of things. He believes that good obtains from specific evils. He thinks it is possible to demonstrate evidentially that the good obtains from the evils occurring on this planet, but one particular evil may itself not be sufficient to bring about the good.

Swinburne postulates that one must look at the larger picture, whether the net gain in human history favors the bad or the good. This is not to say that each evil is not necessary, but that any particular evil may not be sufficient in and of itself to bring about the greater good. Nonetheless, without all of the particular evils, the outweighing good could not obtain. His argument is that the good outweighs the bad, even if only by a little bit. All evil, on the balance of things, is outweighed by the good.

God is fair in allowing the evil because He is the Creator God. Swinburne qualifies this by stating that "God has a right to do something if and only if he does no wrong to anyone else by doing it."[55] Furthermore, no one can claim that God is unfair unless "the bad states were too bad or not ultimately compensated."[56] However, Swinburne adds, "The crucial point is that God must not over time take back as much as he has given. He must remain on balance a benefactor."[57] Swinburne is confident that when put in these terms, the argument demonstrates that the greater good obtains.

If one accepts Swinburne's framework, a question still remains, namely: if God does not know the future choices of His moral agents, how is it that He can be assured that the *greater* good always obtains? If God does not know the evil that men will choose, neither will He know the good they will choose nor how that good might offset some evil. Consider this scenario: A commits a good act (G) at t_1 so that at t_1 God knows about G and does what he can do within the consistency of Himself and the world He created to promote the good that A chooses. At t_2, however, A chooses to use G as an opportunity to choose to do an evil act (E). The question is, if God has only limited knowledge of future choices of his moral creatures, will not God inadvertently promote G, not knowing that G is going to be used to accomplish E? This appears problematic. God, according to Swinburne, is always acting to promote the good or to bring about a greater good out of evil, but He is forced to do so without the benefit of the knowledge of future choices of others that will impact the situation.

Suppose Bill gives Susan, who is in a desperate financial situation, $100 (G). Susan agrees to pay it back in three weeks. However, she chooses to spend her money elsewhere. At the end of three weeks Susan is unable to pay Bill (E). At this point, Bill chooses to forgive the debt (G), but he then chooses to use the forgiveness to coerce Susan to provide him with a sexual favor. Susan senses no way out, so she gives Bill what he wants and loses her virtue (E). Instead of Susan's character being built up (the initial help with the $100), her virtue is destroyed, which can hardly be considered a greater good. According to the limited knowledge scheme, God would have promoted the first good, which in the end was used for evil. This is a reverse of what is often used as an example, but it works both ways. This seems to be a problem for the greater-good justificatory scheme and therefore presents what I believe to be a problem for those like Swinburne who tamper with God's omniscience in order to explain why He allows certain horrific evils. If God does not know about them, He is not responsible for stopping them before they happen.

Natural Evil

Swinburne is to be commended for addressing the matter of natural evil within his theodicy. While I think it comes up short, at least he seriously grapples with an issue that must be addressed in any theodicy. According to Swinburne, natural evil is necessary for man to know how to do evil or good to his fellows; that is, he needs some way of knowing how certain acts will affect those who are the recipient of those acts. "For example, Swinburne writes, "I believe that the occurrence of natural evils (i.e., evils such as disease and accidents unpredictable by humans) is required for humans to have the power to choose between doing significant good or evil to their fellows, for the reason that the observation of the process which produces natural evil is required to do significant evil to their fellows. Without that knowledge the choice between good and evil will not be available."[58] Stump, who has serious reservations about Swinburne's view, points out that Swinburne's major premise rests on the assumption that "men can have knowledge of the consequences of their actions only by induction on the basis of past experience."[59] Past evils are important for man to understand what constitutes suffering so he can avoid or cause the same.

This position, however, does not seem to hold: after man supposedly learns from the natural evil, at that point the natural evil will no longer be necessary, since man will have learned the bad consequences. Yet much of the same natural evil continues.

Swinburne argues continued observation of the evils in nature is necessary. This is part of the greater good because such knowledge is "a further good beyond the mere possession of knowledge."[60] It is not clear at this point if Swinburne is only arguing for the superiority of such knowledge or for the necessity of experience as the sole source of such knowledge. Moreover, what begins as natural evil, once man has gained the practical knowledge from that evil—if he continues in that evil—becomes a moral evil, not a natural evil. This is to ask how can a second person's act of murder be justified, as it is not natural evil but rather moral evil?

Swinburne thinks that some of the most difficult evil happenings can be explained by what he calls the *good-of-being-of-use* approach. At times, someone's suffering is the means by which others are spared the same suffering. "Consider someone hurt or killed in an accident," Swinburne writes: "Where the accident leads to some reform which prevents the occurrence of similar accidents in future (e.g., someone killed in a rail crash which leads to the installation of a new system of railway signaling which prevents similar accidents in future)."[61] This does not give the invitation to someone to do evil so good may come of it, he argues. He appears to qualify his position when he adds: "Nor am I yet passing any judgement about whether the good is as great a good as the bad is bad. Nevertheless, I am claiming, the supreme good of being of use is worth paying the price."[62]

Even with much suffering, Swinburne continues, the fact remains that men still choose to live rather than die, which means that suffering is seldom counted as being so bad one wants to die. What this indicates, Swinburne suggests, is that "even if they think that at present the bad outweighs the good, they live in hope of better times. Thereby they express their belief that a life of good as a whole and over time would be worth having even if its present state is on the balance bad."[63] In the end, he affirms that "God will only cause harm for the sake of good. . . ."[64] This, Swinburne suggests, is evident in the way man looks at life; that is, he believes that in tomorrow lies the hope the good will prevail because this is the way life has proven to be.

Admittedly, Swinburne's efforts to demonstrate inductively from the evidence that gratuitous evil does not exist and the greater good prevails does have merit in some cases. The weakness, however, is revealed once again in that it seems impossible for the theist to demonstrate that the greater good *always* prevails, thus raising a question of legitimacy for the greater-good justificatory framework. Unless it *always* prevails, then the possibility of gratuitous evil exists. Furthermore, the argument is wanting in that it does not make the case that all of this is sufficient moral justification for God to allow the evil. All he has done is show how good might possibly obtain, but has said nothing about whether that good is sufficient to count as moral justification.

When the Good Fails

If life really gets bad (as it appears in some cases), God has the option of bringing death and compensating the individual in the afterlife. Swinburne notes, "If the bad, in particular the suffering, endured by any individual during that period outweighs the good, God does have the power to compensate that individual in an afterlife."[65] This of course would only be an argument if one of the following conditions is met: all men are ultimately saved or all men enjoy some good, albeit at different levels in the life to come. Swinburne hints at the latter when he suggests that "God, being good, would not punish a sinner with a punishment beyond that he deserved; and I suggest that, despite majority Christian tradition, literally everlasting pain would be a punishment beyond the deserts of any human who has sinned for a finite time on Earth."[66] For the incorrigibly wicked soul, Swinburne denies everlasting sensory punishment, rather concluding that "annihilation, the scrap heap, seems an obvious final fate for the corrupt soul."[67] If the wicked are annihilated, it appears the good does not always obtain as Swinburne argues earlier. If the purpose of all suffering is character-building—and for some that never happens, then all the evil in their lives would not have accomplished its purpose, hence that evil would be gratuitous.

Summary

Swinburne has worked to develop a theodicy constructed on the foundation of man's libertarian free will. God will respect the true human freedom where choices really make a difference. To do otherwise would mean God fails His obligations to His creation. In defense of his theodicy, Swinburne addresses different kinds of evil in order to demonstrate evidentially that there are reasons to believe that good always obtains, concluding that gratuitous evil does not exist. God's knowledge is limited when it comes to the future choices of His moral creatures, and God cannot know in advance what a man might do. Swinburne's theodicy unfolds within the context of a world (not necessarily the best world) which has been voluntarily ordered by God. He thinks that a moral evil only occurs when a person knows that the consequences are evil, knowledge which he thinks comes from watching evil in nature. In nature, however, this raises a question about moral accountability for disobeying God's commandments regardless whether the consequences harm someone or not. In the end, I think there are serious theological as well as philosophical issues that bring the sustainability of Swinburne into question.

MICHAEL PETERSON

The third individual to consider is Michael Peterson, who in my estimation, has helped considerably in forwarding the work of developing a theodicy. He suggests that a theodicy should be crafted from a complete Christian worldview and not just from one theological claim that God exists or any other one particular doctrine. As Peterson says, it is rather "asserting a whole set of logically interrelated claims regarding the divine nature and purposes. He (the theist) might even understand the single claim 'God exists' to be invested with this larger interpretative scheme and therefore entailing all sorts of other claims about God's ways with the world."[68] This point made by Peterson is of real significance, especially as we have viewed the different theodicies and what has been noticed is that they all suffer from internal inconsistency. Here, Peterson (whether we agree or not with his final conclusions) puts the issue of theodicy in its proper context, that of a total theistic worldview.

For Peterson, developing a coherent whole is as necessary as answering the primary question of evil. Here I believe Peterson is on to something. The merits of the claim that God exists need to be judged on "how well the overall theistic position fares in comparison to other worldviews, both religious and secular."[69] Consequently, he attempts to address the problem of evil from a broad theistic worldview perspective. He thinks the work of a theodicy is not merely proposing a possible reason why God permits evil, but "to articulate *plausible* or *credible explanations* that rest on theistic truths and insights."[70] Peterson wisely encourages the theist to be conscious of his worldview when doing the work of theodicy. I think Peterson encourages us in the right direction on several levels.

One is his notion of theodicy as fitting into a Christian worldview and second that we are not just offering something that is rational, but something we claim has truth value.

Framing Problem

According to Peterson, many still believe that evil provides a basis for some kind of evidential argument against theism. That is, when one looks at all the evil in this world, it seems to be strong evidence that God does not exist. He notes that "the trick is to arrive at a formulation of an evidential argument from evil that significantly advances the discussion."[71] Peterson admits that this is a difficult but not impossible task as it "asks the theist to make sense of evil in light of his belief in God. In this case, the theist must answer the critic's charge that cites some alleged fact about evil as the *evidence* that supports the conclusion that it is more probable, given the evidence, to believe that God does not exist."[72] He argues, quite correctly I think, that Christians need to provide a plausible or credible explanation for why God allows all this evil in His world.

In order to approach this task in a way that increases the possibility of its success, Peterson identifies three different forms of the evidential argument from evil. He points out three objections the skeptic might present as evidence against God's existence:

(E_1) Evil exists;

(E_2) Large amounts, extreme kinds and perplexing distributions of evil exist;

(E_3) Gratuitous or pointless evil exists.[73]

Different skeptics have thought that all three arguments argue successfully against God. When any one of the three is conjoined with claiming that "God exists," the probability of that claim seems highly questionable.

Peterson thinks that if (E_1) is what the theist must answer, that the theist could have relative success as "theists typically agree that even quite considerable evil can be allowed by a morally perfect deity as long as it is necessary to either bringing about a greater good or preventing a greater evil."[74] He admits that it is a "dubious assumption that God would not allow the existence of any evil whatsoever."[75] Therefore, Peterson suggests that the broad objection to God's existence based on the fact that some evil exists can be rather handily and successfully countered by the theist.

Responding to (E_2), however, presents the theist with a more difficult but not impossible challenge, says Peterson. The substance of the objection in (E_2) is that "it is not the sheer existence of evil per se that counts against the existence of God but the fact that there are so many evils that are very severe and present in patterns defying comprehension."[76] As Peterson mentions, "Some theists have pointed out that this argument rests on the assumption that the theistic deity would allow only certain amounts, kinds, and distributions of evil. Yet it is hard to know how to establish how much evil is *too much* for God to allow."[77] True as this may be, Peterson holds that this still leaves the theist with the Herculean task of demonstrating that every kind of evil as well as the seemingly disproportionate distribution of evil serves some greater good. The assumption is that if the all-good and all-powerful God allows evil; then it must serve some greater purpose no matter how great the evil.

Peterson concludes that the inescapable force of (E_2) is such that "the burden falls upon the shoulders of thinking Christian theists to articulate a concept of God which is more sophisticated and profound than popular theism envisions."[78] In other words, he concludes that it is important to establish a more precise view of God if one is to respond satisfactorily to the atheistic objection related to (E_2). It may be, however, at this point some Christians will question Peterson's view of God, precisely his understanding of God's knowledge. Peterson understands God's knowledge in a way that is very close to that of an *open theist*. An open theist is one who holds that God cannot know the future choices of His moral agents.

Although the evidential argument entailed in (E_2) is forceful, Peterson thinks that the issue of gratuitous evil (E_3) is undoubtedly the most crucial to the theist. He writes: "So, it is gratuitous or pointless evil, if it exists, that provides crucial evidence against the existence of a supremely powerful, wise, and good God."[79] If the *gratuitous evil* objection is answered, this would contribute to a satisfactory solution to (E_2). In order to answer the objection of (E_3), one needs either to demonstrate evidentially that all evil obtains the good (and thus defeat the claim that some evil is gratuitous) or develop a theistic worldview in which gratuitous evil does not count against God.

It seems to me that Peterson's conclusion is on point. If we cannot show that all evil results in some greater good, then what is left is that some evil is gratuitous. In which case, the task is to show that gratuitous evil does not count against the moral character of God. On this point, I think Peterson is precisely on target. He is the first of those we have reviewed who is at least willing to look at the matter of gratuitous evil, and until we do, I would say we will not develop a plausible explanation for why God allows so much evil in this world.

When answering the atheistic objection from gratuitous evil, Peterson maintains that William Rowe[80] presents the most formidable formulation of this version of the problem. He notes: "Rowe's argument has virtually been the paradigm for the evidential argument from evil since the late 1970s."[81] Peterson notes that Rowe's argument begins with the assumption that gratuitous evil exists, which is based upon *prima facie* evidence from the world, and concludes that, therefore, God does not exist. That is, the assumption is that if gratuitous evil exists, then God does not.

It is on this point that Peterson notes the inherent difficulty of the greater-good approach. If God allows only that evil by which the good is ultimately obtained, then it is incumbent upon the theist to demonstrate evidentially that this is so. In light of the fact there appears to be much evil that shows no sign of obtaining the good, then the greater-good approach has answered the more general problem—evil exists (E_1)—but it has exacerbated the problem created by denying gratuitous evil (E_3) as a possibility. It seems to me it would not be necessary for the theist to identify when gratuitous evil happened, only that the possibility gratuitous evil does exist and that it does not count against God's moral nature.

Peterson acknowledges that most theists have approached the problem by trying to "rebut or mitigate the force of Rowe's first premise and thus stop the argument from working."[82] In spite of their efforts the fact remains that the "evidential argument from gratuitous evil is now widely considered the most formidable objection to theistic belief."[83] In fact, Peterson claims that "the most potent atheistic rebuttals to theistic specifications of greater goods revolve around the claim that at least some evils or some kinds of evils do not seem necessary to any greater good."[84] Whereas "theists have typically taken a *greater-good approach* as integral to their search for a morally sufficient reason for why God allows evil,"[85] the theist must either demonstrate evidentially that gratuitous evil does not exist or rethink the *greater-good approach.* According to Feinberg, Peterson thinks "the better approach to solving this problem is not to deny the factual premise, but to admit its truth and to reject the theological premise."[86] The factual premise is that gratuitous evil exists and the theological premise is that God could not (or would not) allow gratuitous evil to exist (meticulous providence).[87]

As Peterson notes, the theist has generally attempted to prove that gratuitous evil does not exist. I agree with Peterson, but I think this has been done by philosophical sleight of hand (circular reasoning and equivocation) as the theist employs a deductive (*a posteriori*) approach to an evidential argument. This approach says that God cannot allow gratuitous evil; therefore, He does not allow gratuitous evil. This is Peterson's point when he says, "One flaw in many theodicies is that they tacitly assume that God exists and then argue against gratuitous evil with this confidence smuggled in. But within the framework of the problem of evil, this is an illicit assumption, since God's existence is the very thing in question."[88] In an attempt to avoid circular reasoning, Peterson addresses the problem of evil by developing a theodicy that acknowledges the existence of gratuitous evil while demonstrating that gratuitous evil does not count against God. He thereby challenges the idea that God would permit evil in His creation only if He would bring some greater good from the evil. Peterson questions this theological notion as unjustified within classical theism. Unfortunately, at least from my view, is that Peterson's argument assumes a position very close to an openness view, which has already been discussed.

Libertarian Freedom

Peterson argues that libertarian freedom makes gratuitous evil a real possibility and then shows how gratuitous evil is a reasonable (not logically necessary) correlative to libertarian freedom. He writes:

> [When we] consider that God chose to create free rational and moral agents who would exist in an independent, stable order—even though this creation en-

50   *Review of Contemporary Theodicies*

tails the possibility of gratuitous evil—we see a God who does not hesitate to permit conditions (e.g., a natural order within which free creatures can significantly operate) under which such goods can be achieved, even though these same conditions may give some men grounds for atheism.[89]

The unfortunate downside of all of this freedom is evils that, by all definitions, are horrendous and repulsive to the moral sensibilities of humanity.

Peterson's point is that "God cannot eliminate the frightening possibility of gratuitous natural evil as long as he chooses to sustain natural order which, in turn, sustains a great many natural and moral goods."[90] That is, for Peterson, the evil comes with the good, and to tamper with the natural law and moral order would seriously compromise man's free will, and, for Peterson, "Free will is most significant—and fitting for the special sort of creature man is—if it includes the potential for utterly damnable choices and actions. This is part of the inherent risk in God's program for man."[91] Peterson on this point echoes the position of Swinburne.

Still, Peterson adheres to the idea that God uses at least some evil to accomplish His soul-making or character-building purposes. Therefore, some evil is justified. But there can only be true soul-making potential from evil if man lives in an environment where he is really free to choose between the good and the evil. This makes this world the only *kind* of a world (not necessarily the best of its kind) that God could create, according to Peterson. It is precisely this kind of world that provides the opportunity for man to develop his moral character. Therefore, on the balance of things, this world (even with its gratuitous evil) is arguably a world that is worth being in existence. The net gain of the greater good makes this creation valuable (a creation where man has libertarian freedom), even though this freedom may result in some gratuitous evil.

In fact he asserts that "a theistic case against gratuitous evil casts grave doubt on the reliability of human experience and on the moral and rational categories which condition it, and thus runs the risk of being self-defeating."[92] This would mean that to deny gratuitous evil would mean casting real doubts on man's libertarian freedom. Peterson is in the Augustinian tradition when he claims that a world where man has real freedom is a better world than one in which he does not have true freedom. This would lead to the idea that gratuitous evil is possible.

I think Peterson is right on this point, but where Peterson goes wrong, or so I think, is how he argues for the possibility of gratuitous evil. For him, gratuitous evil can exist, but not count against God's moral being because God cannot know the future choices of his moral beings. Therefore, He cannot stop that of which He has no knowledge. Here, it seems that Peterson is very close to open theism, a position I would argue raises serious theological questions. You will remember that although Swinburne denied gratuitous evil, he held a similar view of God's omniscience.

God's Omniscience

He defines *omniscience* as "*at any time, God knows all propositions that are true at that time and are such that God's knowing them at that time is logically possible, and God never believes anything that is false.*"[93] The critical point in his definition is "logically possible." According to Peterson, some things are logically impossible for God to know, such as future choices of his free moral creatures. Since such knowledge is logically impossible for God to know, it cannot count against His omniscience. God cannot know the logically impossible any more than He can do the logically impossible. In this way, Peterson affirms that God is omniscient, yet does so in a way that is more consistent with those who hold to the *openness* of God view rather than the view of classical theism.

Gratuitous Evil

According to Peterson, the theist has two options regarding the matter of gratuitous evil. One is to deny the existence of gratuitous evil and argue that it is only *apparent* gratuitous evil. The second is to affirm the actual existence of gratuitous evil (as opposed to only the appearance) and to try to demonstrate it does not count against a morally perfect Being. If the theist elects for the first option (which most G-G theodicists do), then he will need to give some evidential or theological justification about why it is possible to conclude that God accomplishes a greater good from all evil. If, however, the theist claims that gratuitous evil does exist, as Peterson suggests, then the Christian's task is to present a case for why it is philosophically and theologically possible for gratuitous evil to exist and to do so without counting against the character of God.

Peterson thinks that the best approach is not to deny gratuitous evil, but rather to acknowledge its existence and then show that it does not count against the moral perfection or the omnipotence of God. Peterson does not claim that all evil is gratuitous; in fact, he thinks that one can understand God using evil to build moral character in voluntarily responding humans. God does not cause the evil, but by His permitting it, He uses some of it for good. This good, on the balance of things, is valuable enough to make this world (with moral beings having libertarian freedom) a worthwhile creation. On this point, it seems Peterson has argued correctly.

Others are inclined to view Peterson's view of gratuitous evil with guarded approval. Ronald Nash thinks that in light of Peterson's view on the existence of gratuitous evil, there would seem to be "good reasons to conclude that the stalemate is over and that the probabilities favor theism."[94] After examining Peterson's position, Feinberg says, "Moreover, his [Peterson's] handling of gratuitous evil contains interesting subtleties and is most stimulating intellectually. All of this is praiseworthy, and I believe his appeal to the free will defense does justify the existence of much gratuitous evil for one committed to a free will theology like Arminianism."[95] What needs to be shown, if Peterson's view of gratuitous evil is to gain acceptance in broader theological groups, is that his view does not require Arminian theology. This point I think can be made.

Summary

Peterson builds a theodicy on the notion of the libertarian freedom of man. Man is really free to disobey and even choose hell. God's natural law and moral order establish the context within which God works among men. As a rule, He does not interfere with the choices of men, for this would go contrary to the order He has established. Therefore, gratuitous evil exists, but it does not count against God, for to intervene and bring about a good would be going against the way God created the world to be. However, not all evil is gratuitous as God does often bring good out of evil. Whereas God is faithful to His creation, He will not violate the order of free will. Unfortunately, Peterson moves close to the openness of God view as part of his libertarian view of man's freedom—but stops just short of endorsing it. It appears, however, that one need not accept Peterson's view of God's omniscience in order to accept his position on gratuitous evil. Gratefully, what Peterson has put forward does make a significant contribution to the work of theodicy. Its most promising contribution is that it offers an alternative to accepting the basic self-defeating premise of G-G theodicies and acknowledges that gratuitous evil exists without counting against either the goodness or power of God.

CONCLUSION

After considering the three G-G theodicies we see the one thing they have in common is they all affirm human libertarian freedom. On the matter of the greater good as the justification for God allowing evil in this world, Hick and Swinburne affirm it to be the case, while Peterson thinks it only applies to some evil. Hick argues that God uses evil to accomplish the task of soul-making. Whereas God does nothing without purpose, including allowing all kinds of evil, ultimately all souls will be perfected. If perfection is not completed in this life, it will be completed in the life to come. This leads to a view that even Hick admits sounds very much like the idea of purgatory, although he does not call it that. All souls will eventually be perfected, either by the suffering in this life or in the life to come, but in either case it will be efficacious because ultimately all will be perfected. For Hick, the love of God guarantees the end, which is universal salvation—everybody is saved according to Hick's view.

Swinburne builds a G-G theodicy that develops around the libertarian free-will of man and the openness of God. He believes it is logically impossible for God to know what the future decisions of His moral beings will be if man really has freedom to choose. For Swinburne, gratuitous evil does not exist. He seems unclear about the notion of eternal damnation and gestures to a moderating position, but does not specifically state what that is. He gives examples of where good obtains from evil, but fails to argue conclusively that such is true in all cases of evil. For Swinburne, these examples only show how God possibly might use evil.

Peterson, while arguing for a modified soul-making theodicy, affirms a libertarian view of human freedom. His view of libertarian freedom leads him to a position which is very close to the openness view of God's omniscience. It is this view of God's omniscience that, in part, forms his argument for the possibility of gratuitous evil in a way that does not count against God's moral perfection. I think this position opens his position to the most serious criticism; although I agree with his view of libertarian freedom and gratuitous evil, I am not in sympathy with his way of grounding his argument. In addition, he notes that because God is faithful to His creation and His creation order, He will not interfere with the order He has established, even though some of His moral beings turn against Him—and this will result in gratuitous evil. Although God did not design man to choose evil, whereas man did choose evil, God allows man the freedom of choice, and in love provides a way of redemption for those who choose to have their relationship restored to God. He does not hold to any view of universal salivation.

These three main theodicies charted below (see fig. 3.1) summarize the position of each with respect to the key issues that shape one's theodicy and to help compare the different philosophical and theological components of the respective theodicies. The purpose is to give an overview of the philosophical and theological positions held by the three for general understanding only. There is no attempt to suggest that the various theological or philosophical positions are necessary to the respective theodicy.

FIG. 3.1 THREE 'GREATER-GOOD' THEODICIES COMPARED

	John Hick	*Richard Swinburne*	*Michael Peterson*
Fall	Myth	Historic, but not central	Historic
L F	Yes	Yes	Yes
G O	Unclear	Openness	Uncommitted openness
G E	No	No	Yes
BPW	No	No	No
G-G	Yes	Yes	Modified
S-M	Yes	Yes	Yes
Afterlife	Universalism	Annihilation of the wicked	Heaven or Hell

Key:
Fall: As a historic event where men fell from a pristine state, to a sinful state
L F: Libertarian Freedom
G O: God's Omniscience
G E: Gratuitous Evil
BPW: The Best of all Possible Worlds
G-G: Some form of greater good as part of the theodicy
S-M: Some element of soul-making as part of the theodicy
Afterlife: What happens to the perfected soul and the corrupt soul at death

NOTES

1. John Hick, *Evil and the God of Love*, rev. ed. (San Francisco: Harper & Row, 1978), 211–2.
2. John Hick, "An Irenaean Theodicy," in *Encountering Evil*, ed. Stephen T. Davis (Atlanta: John Knox Press, 1981), 42.
3. In fairness to Hick, the most we can say is that he agrees in principle with Irenaeus because Hick admits that the distinction between 'image' and 'likeness' is "exegetically dubious." Hick, *Evil and the God of Love*, 254.
4. Ibid., 257.
5. Ibid., 256.
6. Ibid., 255.
7. Hick, *Evil and the God of Love*, 255.
8. Ibid., 254.
9. Ibid., 259.
10. Ibid., 255.
11. Marilyn McCord Adams and Robert Merrihew Adams, "Introduction," eds. *The Problem of Evil* (Oxford: Oxford University Press, 1990), 18.
12. Hick, *Evil and the God of Love*, 272.
13. Ibid., 273.
14. Hick, *Evil and the God of Love*, 281.
15. Ibid.
16. Ibid.
17. Ibid.
18. Hick, *Evil and the God of Love*, 330.
19. Ibid., 331.
20. Ibid., 361.
21. Hans Schwarz, *Evil: A Historical and Theological Perspective*, trans. Mark W. Worthing (Minneapolis: Fortress Press, 1995), 203.
22. Hick, *Evil and the God of Love*, 335.
23. Ibid., 176.
24. Ibid., 375.
25. Ibid., 333–4.
26. Hick, "An Irenaean Theodicy," 50.
27. Hick, *Evil and the God of Love*, 336.
28. Ibid., 342.
29. Ibid., 347.
30. Ibid.
31. John Hick, *Death and Eternal Life* (New York: Harper & Row Publishers, 1976), 456.
32. Stephen T. Davis, "The Problem of Evil in Recent Philosophy," *Review and Expositor* 82 (Fall 1985): 542.
33. G. Stanley Kane, "The Failure of Soul-Making Theodicy," *International Journal for Philosophy of Religion* 6 (Spring 1975): 2.
34. Schwarz, *Evil*, 203.
35. R. Douglas Geivett, *Evil and the Evidence for God* (Philadelphia: Temple University Press), 226.

36. Barry Whitney, *What Are They Saying About God and Evil?* (New York: Paulist Press, 1989), 43.
37. Richard Swinburne, *Providence and the Problem of Evil* (Oxford: Clarendon Press, 1998), x.
38. Ibid., xii.
39. On this point, he thinks that Plantinga misses the traditional use of 'theodicy' and makes an unwarranted distinction between 'theodicy' and 'defense'.
40. Swinburne, *Providence and the Problem of Evil*, 35.
41. Ibid.
42. Ibid.
43. Philip L. Quinn notes that in the Free Will Defense (which he claims is the position of both Swinburne and Plantinga), that "its key idea is that moral good cannot exist apart from libertarian free actions that are not causally determined." "Philosophy of Religion," in *The Cambridge Dictionary of Philosophy,* ed. Robert Audi (Cambridge: Cambridge University Press, 1995), 611.
44. Swinburne, *Providence and the Problem of Evil*, 35.
45. Ibid., 33–34.
46. Ibid., 34.
47. The compatibilist position maintains that man's freedom and God's determinative sovereignty are compatible.
48. Ibid., 34.
49. Ibid., 32.
50. Ibid., 232–3.
51. Ibid., 3.
52. Ibid., 3.
53. Jerry Walls, "Will God Change His Mind? Eternal Hell and the Ninevites," in *Through No Fault of Their Own?* eds. William V. Crockett and James C. Sigountos (Grand Rapids: Baker Book House Company, 1991), 66.
54. Richard Swinburne, *The Coherence of Theism* (Oxford: Clarendon Press, 1977), 176.
55. Ibid., 223.
56. Ibid., 236.
57. Ibid., 230–31.
58. Richard Swinburne, "Some Major Strands of Theodicy," in *The Evidential Argument From Evil*. Daniel Howard-Snyder, ed. (Bloomington: Indiana University Press, 1996), 31–2.
59. Eleonore Stump, "Knowledge, Freedom, and the Problem of Evil," in *The Problem of Evil*, ed. Michael L. Peterson (Notre Dame: University of Notre Dame Press, 1992), 321.
60. Swinburne, *Providence and the Problem of Evil*, 66.
61. Ibid., 103.
62. Ibid.
63. Ibid., 241.
64. Ibid., 231.
65. Ibid., 233.
66. Richard Swinburne, *Responsibility and Atonement* (Oxford: Clarendon Press, 1989), 181.
67. Ibid.
68. Peterson, *God and Evil*, 87.

69. Ibid., 105.
70. Ibid., 85.
71. Ibid., 67.
72. Ibid., 69.
73. Ibid., 24.
74. Peterson, *God and Evil*, 72.
75. Michael Peterson, *Evil and the Christian God* (Grand Rapids: Baker Book House, 1982), 69.
76. Peterson, *God and Evil*, 71.
77. Ibid.
78. Peterson, *Evil and the Christian God*, 72.
79. Peterson, *God and Evil*, 72.
80. William Rowe, "The Evidential Argument from Evil: A Second Look" in *The Evidential Argument from Evil*, Daniel Howard-Snyder, ed. (Bloomington: Indiana University Press, 1996), 262, notes: "My purpose here is to look again at an evidential argument from evil that I first presented in 1979. Since that time I have made several changes in that argument in an effort to make it clearer and to patch up weakness in earlier statements of it." The formulation of this argument appeared first as "The Problem of Evil and Some Varieties of Atheism," *American Philosophical Quarterly*, 16 (1979), 335–41. In this article he uses as his example for pointless suffering the case where a fawn (Bambi) is trapped in a forest fire and dies an awful, lingering death. Later, he revisits this subject, and it is in this article that he uses as his example of pointless suffering, a five-year old girl (Sue) who is raped, beaten and killed by strangulation.
81. Peterson, *God and Evil*, 74.
82. Ibid., 74.
83. Ibid., 85.
84. Ibid., 104.
85. Ibid., 103.
86. John S. Feinberg, *Many Faces of Evil: Theological Systems and the Problems of Evil* (Wheaton: Crossway Books, 2004), 264.
87. The principle of *meticulous providence* means that God does not allow gratuitous evil. According to Peterson, this principle in the end forces the theist to claim that there is no gratuitous evil, which contradicts the evidence from experience.
88. Peterson, *Evil and the Christian God*, 86.
89. Ibid., 122.
90. Ibid., 116.
91. Ibid., 104.
92. Ibid., 92.
93. Michael Peterson, et al, eds. *Reason and Religious Belief* 2nd ed. (New York: Oxford Press, 1998), 73.
94. Ronald Nash, *Faith and Reason* (Grand Rapids: Zondervan Publishing House, 1988), 221.
95. Feinberg, *The Many Faces of Evil*, 269.

4
WHY GREATER-GOOD THEODICIES FAIL

In this chapter I will critique G-G theodicies, but in doing so, I do not wish to sound either arrogant or dismissive of the work of others. I will, in the interest of clarity, be straightforward in my remarks. I do not wish, however, for any of my remarks to be taken as a personal attack on any individual or her Christianity. I do, however, think that the general premise of all G-G theodicies is wrong, namely that gratuitous evil is not possible within a Trinitarian theistic worldview.

Therefore, I think that gratuitous evil does in fact present evangelicals with the greatest challenge to any greater-good response to evil. As David O'Conner points out, "There is a great deal of evil in the world, much of it seemingly pointless. Intuitively, then, there seems to be a discordance between certain facts of inscrutable evil and the theistic conception of the world as God-made."[1] Horrific evil (which is what seems gratuitous) is precisely the greatest challenge to G-G theodicies. It requires the theist to demonstrate that the good obtains in order to retain the belief that gratuitous evil does not exist.

The difficulty of this task of demonstrating the greater good is reflected in the many varied attempts at proving the good obtains from all evil, including the horrific evils, some of which we looked at in the last chapter. The idea that the only evil allowed by God is the evil from which He can bring about a greater good or prevent a greater evil necessarily requires the rejection of the notion that some evil is gratuitous. It will be argued, however, that it is this very premise that is the seed of destruction internal to G-G theodicies. A more fruitful approach appears to be what Peterson suggests, namely a theodicy that does not depend on the greater-good assumption. Before offering such a proposal, this chapter will examine the greater-good assumption itself and suggest a list of weaknesses inherent in the concept, weaknesses so damaging that in my estimation require abandoning the G-G theodicy altogether.

THE WORK OF THEODICY

It appears that the theist has two options regarding the evidential version of the problem of evil. First, the theist can deny the reality of gratuitous evil, thereby preserving God's moral goodness and power by emphasizing His absolute sovereignty over His creation. At this point, I remind the reader to review the definition of *sovereignty* given in the first chapter to help in understanding where I think many go astray when appealing to God's sovereignty in this argument. I suggest that many see God's sovereignty in such a way that His will is always accomplished on this earth in all the details of life. Application of *sovereignty* in this way supports the claim the all-good, all-powerful God does not allow any evil for which He does not bring some greater good or prevent some greater evil. As I will argue in this chapter, that means when the logic is followed, God is responsible for the evil in this world. I find that conclusion unacceptable in light of the claim of the apostle John when he explains "God is light and in him is no darkness at all" (1 Jn 1:5).

Since the non-existence of gratuitous evil is precisely the point to be proven, to assume the conclusion in the premise involves circular reasoning. Arguing that evil does not count against God because God cannot permit gratuitous evil is circuitous. From a logical point of view, this weakens the force of the argument and existentially causes it to run contrary to the intuitive impulses of man. If we intuitively believed that all evil brought some overriding good, then there would be no impulse to ask why God allowed the evil. That is, if the structure of our world was such that it was fact that God only allowed evil to bring about good, then that is the way we would believe. Just as we believe other things about our world without asking questions. For example, when we throw a ball up in the air and it hits us on the head, we do not ask why the ball came down—it is just the way the world is. Even so, if men intuitively believed that all evil is for some good, there would not be no the question, "God, why this evil?"

Of course, there are two ways to ask the "Why?"question. One way is what we might call the scientific question, a question that helps us to understand how the world works. The other way, which is the way we ask the question when it comes to evil, is the existential question—God, why are you letting this happen? The former is about the operation of nature that inquires into the operation, the latter is about the motive of a personal being, God. These are two different kinds of "Why?" questions.

The atheist concludes that the personal God has no moral justification for allowing the evil, and hence concludes God does not exist. It seems rather weightless simply to reply to the atheist that he has no argument against God because without God the atheist has no explanation for good. The point being made is that without God, there is no way to judge between good and bad events.

While this may be true, it hardly meets the challenge of asking why God, if He exists, allows evil. As Christians we affirm both the existence of evil and the existence of God, and it is within that context that we must answer the "Why?"

question. If we, as Christians, affirm both the existence of God and the reality of evil, how we answer the "Why?" question, cannot be addressed by merely redirecting the question. Therefore, we must find a way to answer how both those affirmations can be reconciled without a redefinition of either or a denial of one or the other.

As Peterson points out, the serious challenge from the atheist is not that there is some evil in the world, but that there is so much evil, and some of it is so terrible. It seems that the Free-Will argument seems satisfactory to explain why there is evil in God's creation in the first place, namely, evil is the consequent (not necessary consequent) of God giving man libertarian freedom. The more pressing problem, however, is why evil seems so pervasive and destructive to humanity if a loving and omnipotent God is in control. That is, why does God continue to allow such evil when He clearly has the power to stop it?

We must not forget the true essence of the question before us. If we do, we will end up answering the question that is not being asked. On the other hand, the answer to the real question, namely that God only allows the evil from which He can bring about a greater good or prevent a greater evil, may answer the question, but in doing so, places a tremendous (and I would say unnecessary) evidentiary burden on the theist. We must not forget that the burden of proof belongs to the one who makes the claim. In this case, the burden of proof belongs to the theist since he is the one who makes the claim—God exists.

GREATER-GOOD PREMISE UNDER THE MICROSCOPE

I will now look at what I think are some serious questions that the greater-good premise raises. I realize that simply raising questions does not prove the position is wrong. It may be that someone replies by saying that I have misunderstood the position of G-G theodicies. You the reader will have to be the judge there. I have tried to give a fair accounting of major G-G theodicies so that you can judge for yourself. Others may complain that asking the question of God on this matter is only my rational arrogance. To that, I would answer that I am not asking the question because I think I have caught God in a moral lapse, but rather I ask the question because I believe there is an answer. I believe that the God of revelation has not intended that we ignore this great question, nor does He expect that we merely place the question in the category of *mystery*. I think intellectual honesty and Christian integrity requires us to wrestle with this question until we come to a better understanding.

Evil: Necessary or Incidental

Let me begin by raising a very fundamental question. If God uses all evil for good (the general premise of the greater good), then the question remains: Is the evil only *incidental* to the good or *necessary* for the good? Let's follow the logic of this question. If the evil (consider the little girl raped and buried alive) is *inci-*

dental to the good, then the theist must show that God is justified in permitting something so horrific when it is only *incidental* to the good. By *incidental* I mean that the world does not need that particular good that comes from the evil. In this case it would be gratuitous evil and it means that the good did not need the evil. In this case God allows evil, but the good could have obtained without the evil. If, on the other hand, the evil is *necessary* for the good, then the theist has a whole new set of problems—to demonstrate that the good could not have come about without the existence of that particular evil in this world. If there is a necessary good that can only obtain through God using evil, then it appears there is something omnipotence cannot do, namely, bring about a necessary good without evil. Furthermore, if the good is necessary to the plan of God, then so is the evil, which logically leads to the conclusion that God wills the evil. Denial of this conclusion seems difficult to support.

Moreover, if the good is the character-building or some other category of good, without a particular evil that good would never be present in God's world. This would make something of goodness in this world, at least in part, dependent on a particular evil. It seems reasonable to argue given this position that a world with more *goods* is better than a world without those goods, meaning that a world without evil would also be a world without those goods. Either way one looks at this, if these goods can only come by way of an evil, then it is evil that makes a better world than what otherwise could have been.

Furthermore, if God could have brought about those goods by His power alone, then the question remains, why did He not do it that way? In fact, it would seem that a morally perfect being would bring about the good without the evil. In the end this seems like a difficult position to maintain as it seriously erodes the very point assumed, namely that God is all-powerful and all-good. So, it seems the question still remains: God, why this evil?

In the end, the logic of the greater-good position makes the good necessary which in turn makes the evil necessary. If the evil is necessary to this world and it is God's creation, this makes evil necessary to the plan and purpose of God. At this point, it is difficult if not impossible to escape the conclusion that God is not only responsible for evil, He actually planned the evil—it is His will. If God wills evil while at the same time condemning evil, God acts contrary to Himself, and at that point, all of Christianity collapses.

What is meant by God's Sovereignty?

The difficulty of demonstrating evidentially the actuality of the greater-good premise has not been lost on some theists. Some maintain the position based upon the fact of God's sovereignty. God is sovereign in such a way that all individual choices of men are only those which God directly permits. His plan is such that it includes the evil, and this is all that is needed in terms of a theodicy. This solution appeals to God's sovereignty as the basis for the G-G theodicy and is an *inferential argument*. There is nothing wrong with inferential arguments as long as there is sufficient warrant to support the claim drawn from the evidence.

In this case, the claim is that there is no gratuitous evil in this world because if there were, it would mean God is not sovereign. That is, so the argument goes, if God is sovereign, then everything has a purpose, including evil. The scriptural evidence is the numerous Scriptures that speak of God as the Sovereign One. There is no objection to the claim that God is sovereign, as the Bible is clear on this matter. The question is whether or not the understanding of *sovereignty* means that everything that happens on this earth has a purpose, which is the often expressed in the phrase, "God is in control."

First, some confusion exists among Christians as how *sovereignty* should be defined. As Peterson observed, Christians must work for more precise definitions when speaking of God. *Sovereignty* is often used interchangeably with *providence* and *omnipotence*. Clearly, the three terms do not speak of the same attribute of God. In fact, providence does not appear to be an attribute of God, but rather the way in which God acts because He is God. God's providence has to do with His daily governance over His creation. *Sovereignty* can best be defined as divine autonomy.

Because God is sovereign, He is the supreme ruler since all His pre-creation and creation choices were not influenced by anyone or anything outside of Himself. God's choice to create and to create the way He did, as well as His counsels concerning the operation and end of creation, are solely His choices (Is 45–6). Here God affirms that whatever He has planned He will do (Is 46:10). These verses do not say that He has willed everything that happens on this earth, but what He has planned, no human can thwart—it will come to pass. What His sovereignty chooses, His omnipotence perfects. *Omnipotence* relates to the extent and kind of God's power. There is no person or thing that has more power than God. He is all-powerful not because He can do anything (such as the logically impossible), but because His power is circumscribed by none. While these three terms are connected, they are not interchangeable.

Second, how should *sovereignty* be applied in the case of gratuitous evil? Does it necessarily mean that if something happens on this earth without a divine purpose, this somehow strikes at the truth of God's sovereignty? It seems to me that the answer is *No*; to maintain otherwise leads to questionable ends. For example, say a person commits adultery: is it gratuitous evil or is it an evil that God in His sovereignty planned? The plan would have had to be from before creation or at the moment of creation. The end is that God planned for a person to commit adultery, the very thing that God says is sin. God becomes the author of sin. Furthermore, the adultery was planned to bring about a good (under the G-G theodicy), so now sin brings about good and it could be argued that more sin would bring about more good. In principle this is the very conclusion the Apostle Paul rejects (Ro 6:1–2).

In the end, if this is how sovereignty is defined and applied, it collides with other non-negotiable doctrines of Christianity. When we see sovereignty (as shown in the previous paragraphs), it teaches that everything that happens on this earth is God's will. That makes not only the good that obtains God's will, but the evil which was necessary for the good to obtain as the will of God.

I would also like to point out that there are two legitimate ways to understand God's sovereignty as it works in time and space. One often hears this expressed in terms that God is in control of history. However, that can be understood in as meaning He controls by determining all particular acts of men. This would be like saying that a man is in control of his automobile. When he turns the steering wheel to the left, the car moves to the left (assuming the mechanism is working properly and the automobile is in motion). There is, however, another way of understanding *control,* which is revealed in the statement "The father is in control of his house." Here we simply mean that he has laid down rules or guidelines for the different members of the family and sees to it that all activity falls within those guidelines. In this sense, we speak of *control* in a slightly different way. I will suggest that the second sense is more in line with the biblical record.

Lastly, some would want to argue that if everything does not have a purpose, then we end up with chaos. But is that really the case? I think the answer is *No.* What is missed here is the distinction between reason and purpose. I would argue that everything that happens on this planet has a reason and therefore is not chaotic, although not everything necessarily has a purpose. In chapter one I referred to this point and gave an example which I will repeat here. I think this helps us to understand the difference.

Consider that you come to me and ask me why I did not pay my electric bill last month. Suppose I say to you that it is because I am protesting the recent increase in electric rates. In that case I am giving you my purpose in not paying my electric bill (of course, you can also say it is a reason—true, but my main point is *purpose.* However, suppose I respond to your question by saying that I did not pay my bill because I simply did not have the money. Now I have given you a reason, but not a purpose. So, the fact that I did not pay my electric bill in both cases is such that it is not a chaotic event, even though in the second instance, there is not some purpose.

I would argue that there is always a reason why everything happens in human history, but not all things that happen do so because they serve some purpose. Hence, in the subject before us, there is always a reason for every evil, but there is not necessarily a purpose (say the greater good). In both cases, God is still sovereign and events in human history are not chaotic nor by chance.

The Good is Beyond Our Ken

One of the serious challenges to the greater-good model is in explaining the *good* when no one can see it. For example, where is the good when the little girl is abducted, raped and buried alive? Some theists such as Stephen Wykstra argue that in all cases the good does obtain from evil, but in some cases, the good is beyond man's ken (that is, beyond man's range of vision or knowledge/understanding). He defends this position in his response to the challenge of William Rowe (you will remember he was discussed earlier in this volume). His objection to Rowe's argument turns on Rowe's appeal to the fact that one often does not see all evil resulting in some greater good. Wykstra, however, argues that Rowe fails to understand that just because we do not see it, does not mean the evil that results in a greater good will never come to pass. To make his point, Wykstra turns to the principle of the Condition of Reasonable Epistemic Access (CORNEA). According to Wykstra,

> CORNEA says that we can argue from 'we see no X' to 'there is no 'X' only when X has 'reasonable seeability'—that is, is the sort of thing which, if it exists we *can reasonably expect* to see it in the situation. Looking around in my garage and seeing no dog entitles me to conclude that none is present, but seeing no flea does not; and this is because fleas, unlike dogs, have low seeability; even if they were present, we cannot reasonably expect to see them in this way. But should we expect God-purposed goods to have the needed seeability? Arguing from the disparity between a creator's vision and ours, I urge not: Rowe's case thus fails CORNEA's seeability requirement.[2]

Wykstra's argument is rather straightforward. God sees things differently than man sees them, and this is what one would expect given that God is infinite and man is finite (Is 55:8–9—verses often quoted to support this position). I would respond by saying that just because His ways are higher than ours does not mean they cannot be known. I think it is somewhat missing the point of the text. It is not that they are out of sight, but rather they operate at a much higher level. Wykstra's point is that the "seeability" of the good which comes from some evil is such that one would not expect man to see it even if it were present. God brings the good from the evil. Whereas God's ways are not man's ways, it is reasonable that the good would be beyond man's ken, or so argues Wykstra. Therefore, the good is present, but under the circumstances one should not expect to see it. Consequently, one should not conclude that just because he does not see the good that there is no good—only God can see it. Therefore, there is no justification for denying its reality.

In order to judge the acceptability of Wykstra's argument, we must determine in what way *appearance* is different for God than it is for man. First, there is no argument that God sees matters more comprehensively than man because He knows all things. What must be demonstrated is that God sees things differently than man, and that this fact applies in the case of evil where the good obtains but is not seen. Of course, the question then remains under what assumption are we better to affirm it if we cannot see it. Furthermore, is it simply a matter of seeing or knowing or is something else involved?

As I see it, there are three possible ways to understand Wykstra's idea. One, God sees the good, while man does not see it because the good obtains by God's intervention and only God knows how He will intervene in order to bring about the good. This refers to how the good obtains. Two, God sees the good and man does not because God knows that the good will obtain. In this case, He sees farther into the future and thereby sees what man does not see in the flow of natural order. God is in eternity and man is in time. Three, God sees good differently than man sees good. This is an issue of definition.

If it is the first possibility, then the problem of man's seeing is still not solved, for if it is just a matter of means, eventually the good would still become evident and man would see it. If it is the second, and the good is far down the road, then when the good does obtain, some man would see it. If it is so far down the road that the person who suffered is not the one rewarded, then this would seem to be an abrogation of the scriptural principle of reward and recompense. The one who suffers should also be the one who sees the good. Furthermore, if it is so far removed from the suffering, how can one be sure that the good comes from the evil? If it is the third, then God sees *good* differently than man, which raises the question of how man knows when he has done good as God sees it—that is, if God defines *good* differently than man. In fact, one might argue that this could lead to a terrible confusion between what is called *good* and what is called *evil*. Whereas God is the One man is to please, not understanding *good* as God does would leave man always wondering if he had done good. Furthermore, if man and God understand *good* differently, then religious language is equivocal, throwing all communication between man and God into confusion.

Two other observations seem to call Wykstra's solution into question. The first is his example of seeabilty under the principle of CORNEA. In his example, not seeing the flea is not an epistemological problem, but an ontological one— the size of the flea against that of the dog. Fleas do have seeability, but Wykstra's reasoning is actually trying to defend *no seeability* for his argument is that we cannot see the good as we cannot see the flea. It appears that he has engaged in the fallacy of *false analogy*. This is not to say that an example cannot be given, but the one he gives seems to miss the mark. It is not the size of the good that keeps man from seeing it, but something else. The reason Wykstra does not see the flea in the garage is because of the size of the flea, not his cognitive powers. If he looked really hard, it would be possible to see the flea even in a garage because it *does* have seeability, albeit rather low.

Following Wykstra's analogy, the good obtained from evil could be seen; it would simply mean that one would have to look harder to see it. In addition, it would seem that if the evil was a really big evil, then in order for the good to outweigh the evil, it too would have to be a rather large good, in which case one wonders how it could be missed. Even if one grants Wykstra his point that God sees things differently than man, what follows is a concern about other areas of life. Do theists also suggest that God sees justice or morality differently than man? This may not be a strong concern, but it needs to be addressed. Why should suffering be the only aspect of life that falls into this category if this is the way God works?

The second observation concerns Wykstra's complaint that Rowe's examples are prejudiced in Rowe's favor (his examples are too difficult). One could not deny this, but it would only be a legitimate objection if, in fact, Rowe uses an example bearing no consistency with reality. The fact is if the example is within the range of human experience, Rowe has every right to introduce it. In fact, there are many cases in everyday life that are similar to Rowe's example of the young girl being horribly abused (as I have mentioned earlier). It is just these kinds of evil that raise the question from the atheist—where is the good? Or, God, why this evil? Therefore, Wykstra's argument seems to fail on several counts (or it is at least suspect in that it begs the question). Consequently, it seems to me that this explanation is little help to those who wish to hold on to a greater-good justificatory framework in response to the argument from evil.

All Things Work Together For Good

It seems to me that trying to justify the greater-good explanation on grounds of the physical/psychological evidence is a very unconvincing project. Certainly the argument that the good is beyond our ken (however, you define 'ken,') the argument is indeed weightless and far from being compelling. What would put the case for G-G theodicies in a very strong position would be an unambiguous propositional statement in the Bible affirming its premise. According to some theists, such a verse is Romans 8:28. This verse affirms that "all things work together for good to those who love God and are called according to His purpose." Does this verse teach that God brings good out of all evil? I would say no. Several exegetical matters are crucial to understanding the force of this text and what it has to say regarding evil (suffering) in this world.

First, the context limits the benefits of the statement to believers only, and specifically limits the good to those who love God. Even if one takes "to love God" in its broadest possible meaning to include all true Christians, it still fails to support the weight placed on it. Consider for argument's sake: if it were true that, in the general flow of things, all suffering turned out for one's good, then why tell the Christian it is true only for those who love God? The fact that believers are singled out indicates that the principle is particular to them and no one else. No matter how one defines good or when one claims the good obtains—this life or in the life to come—this verse does not teach that all evil (natural, moral, and physical) turns into some good.

In addition, I would argue that the context of Romans 8 speaks to suffering that comes to the Christian as result of his righteous living. Romans 8:28 is bookended by verse 17: "heirs of God and joint heirs with Christ, if indeed we suffer with Him," and verse 36: "For Your (God's) sake we are killed all the day long; we are counted as sheep for the slaughter." The groaning of all creation, including man, does not explain our suffering, but rather in what state we remain as we wait for the Day of redemption—that is when the "glory is going to be revealed in us" (19). The force of the Romans 8 text is that we should live boldly for God, knowing no resulting form of suffering can separate us from the love of God that is in Christ Jesus our Lord (Ro 8:37–39), so we should remain faithful at all costs.

This understanding of Romans 8:28 is in harmony with other biblical texts that speak of Christian suffering, such as Matthew 5:11 ("for My sake"); 2 Timothy 3:12 ("desire to live godly"); James 1:3 ("the testing of your faith"); and 1 Peter 1:7 ("genuineness of your faith"). Furthermore, consider the following examples: Job suffered because of his righteousness (Job 1:10); Joseph, because of his faithful proclamation of God's dreams to him (Gen 37:19—"Look, this dreamer is coming"); Shadrach, Meshach, and Abed-Nego for not worshiping the gold image (Dan 3:8–25); and Daniel for praying to God (Dan 6:10–23). When Christians suffer for righteousness sake, God is at work to work things together for ultimate good for those in the Kingdom.

One thing we learn from this is that the good obtains *in spite of* the evil, not *because of* the evil. That is not to suggest there in no hope for the Christian in his suffering, but that comes from another text. According to 2 Corinthians 1:3–7, Christians can be assured that the Father of mercies and God of all comfort is present to encourage and comfort them in their time of suffering. 2 Corinthians 12:9 reminds the Christian that God's grace is always sufficient for all situations even when we suffer because we live in a fallen world.

Another verse often introduced into the discussion is Genesis 50:20, which records Joseph's response to his brothers when he finally reveals his true identity to them. You remember that they were obviously afraid that Joseph would exercise retribution on them. Joseph sees the fear in their eyes and comforts them. In reply, Joseph reassures them he has no intention of avenging their dastardly deed of selling him into slavery many years before. He says, "But as for you, you meant evil against me; God meant it for good in order to bring it about as it is today, to save many people alive" (Gen 50:20). This text only tells what happened in this particular circumstance, and it is unwise to build a doctrine on a strictly narrative text as there is nothing normative about the text. In this case, God does allow Joseph's evil treatment by his brothers to get Joseph to Egypt. It does not say that God caused the brothers to do this, but as they did it, God was at work to bring about a good end. In Genesis 45, Joseph says, "But now, do not be angry with yourselves because you sold me here; for God sent me before you to preserve life (v. 5).

Once again, all we have here is Joseph's testimony, which is, after the fact, about how God reversed the evil plans of his brothers and that God was at work in this situation for a greater purpose. I do not deny that God does such things—not as the rule, but as the exception. Furthermore, we only know it was this way because God reveals it. In addition, it seems quite clear that Joseph's evil treatment from his brothers resulted from his righteousness—they called him the dreamer because he had told them of God's nighttime visions. Also, Joseph makes no mention of the other suffering he encountered while in Egypt such as being thrown in prison and that that had somehow brought about a greater good. He only mentions the matter of the evil deed of his brothers.

If these conclusions are right, there is no propositional statement affirming the greater-good assumption for all kinds of evil on this earth. What we do have is God's promise to His children that no matter what happens on this earth, He never leaves us nor forsakes us and through it all is always at work in our lives for the good of His Kingdom. I might point out further that neither Romans 8:28 or Genesis 50:20 say anything about natural or physical evil.

Evil is Necessary to the Good

Arguing that God allows only that evil from which He can bring about a greater good when the logic is followed inevitably leads to some rather unacceptable conclusions. What assumptions must be true in order to accept this affirmation and what are the logical conclusions if they are true? Peterson wisely argues that any solution to the problem of evil should not be done in theological isolation. The theist must make sure that whatever answer he gives is consistent with a complete Christian worldview. What is said about God in relation to evil will have implications for most other major doctrines of Protestant orthodoxy.

First, it is posited that God allows all evil that comes into the world because from it He will bring about some greater good. Remember, we have discounted the part about preventing a worse evil as it is only a guess. The question I want to pose is: Is the good that God brings from the evil a necessary good or not? Is this good essential to God's plan for humanity or is it just a good that happens because the evil is allowed, making the good incidental to God's plan for humanity? It seems the only consistent answer is that it is necessary to the plan of God. If not, why allow all the suffering if the plan of God would be just as complete without the resulting good? So, what are the implications of this for the theist?

If the good is necessary, then so is the particular evil, for if the good could be accomplished with a lesser evil, then the all-good God would use the lesser evil. The end is, that that particular evil is necessary, for the good could not obtain without the evil and the good must obtain because it is necessary. If the good is necessary, and it is dependent on the evil, then the evil must also be necessary. If the evil is necessary, I see little hope of escaping the conclusion that God must have determined the evil. Otherwise, there could be no assurance that there would be the good. As we have seen before, this makes God directly responsible for the evil—not in a contingent way, but in a necessary way.

There is no evidential proof that certain evil is *necessary* to a corollary good, or that *all* evil always obtains a greater good. To claim such is the case seems far beyond the preponderance of the evidence.[3] In fact, it is impossible to prove that the evil is necessary to the good just because good comes from the evil, any more than it is possible to make the case that the particular good is necessary. This mistake in logic assumes that just because B follows A there is necessarily some causal relationship between A and B. Further, it openly confesses that what *is* constitutes what *ought* to have been or even *must* be.

It is obvious that there is a large difference between claiming that good comes from evil and arguing that the evil is *necessary* to the good. It may be possible, at least in some cases, to demonstrate that good comes from evil. However, it is a very different task to argue that evil is necessary to the good. If one argues that the good is not necessary, then the G-G theodicy must respond to why God allows such suffering for something that is not necessary. What happens in the end is that the appeal to God's sovereignty and power as the grounds for supporting the greater-good assumption actually undermines those very attributes the G-G theodicy seeks to protect. God needs the evil in order to accomplish the good, which says, God cannot accomplish the good without the evil, making God's plan dependent on evil. If God can bring about the good without the evil, then it seems that is what the all-good, all-powerful God would do.

The End Justifies the Means

Another suggested logical conclusion of the greater-good premise is that it promotes a type of argument that turns on the end-justifies-the-means philosophy. As R. Z. Friedman says, "The end, in other words, justifies the means. Yet this is the complete antithesis of the moral task which religion gives to God."[4] Norman Geisler counters this argument[5] when he writes that the "theist does not say that a good end justifies God's *performing* evil acts, but it only justifies God's *permitting* such acts."[6] He goes on to say that "God is interested in bringing the greatest good for the greatest number, but not at the expense of performing or promoting any evil."[7] The argument, however, is not that God *performs* evil only that He allows it. If God allows evil to bring about a greater good, then the end is the good and the means is the evil, and this seems to me to fit the notion of the end justifies the means.

This argument maintains that the good comes from this or that evil and that the good would not exist apart from this or that evil. If God is omnipotent and omni-benevolent, then what He permits must be the best because He can prevent what is not best. In such a case, evil becomes the path to good, so it would seem the best action would be to let evil runs its course, for in the end it will be good.

In this vein, Friedman's observations seem proper: "As an individual in possession of the knowledge of good and evil I ought to act to alleviate the suffering of the innocent, but as a theodicist perhaps I ought to accept the power of evil to produce good and allow the process to run its course without my 'interference'."[8] He goes on to say, "The theodicist's claim that evil produces good and is therefore not really a challenge to the existence of and goodness of God may undermine the claim, central to that tradition which gives rise to this defense of God, that man knows the difference between good and evil."[9] His point is that, in the end, there is no difference between good and evil because out of evil comes good. Richard Middleton agrees. He notes, "If the greater good defense is true, although we might feel sorrow over these events [Bosnia, Rawanda, Auschwitz and Dachau] when viewed in isolation, nevertheless we ought ultimately to praise God for them, since seen in their proper perspective they are necessary to some greater good which could not be accomplished without them."[10] If Middleton's observations are correct, this creates no small amount of theological tension, as it logically leads to the position that evil must be left unrestrained if the good is to obtain.

Again, Middleton raises the point, "If the greater good defense were truly believed, it would undercut motivation for both petitionary prayer and redemptive opposition to evil by generating a self-deceptive apathy instead of a biblically inflamed passion for justice and shalom."[11] Moreover, Friedman thinks that since "the logic of theodicy may force us there, we find ourselves in direct conflict with the view of moral agency contained in the Fall, that man having eaten of the forbidden tree is in possession of the knowledge of good and evil."[12]

Those who hold to a greater-good premise can protest strenuously against this conclusion. Yet, it seems this is very much a case of the end justifying the means. In the end, the G-G theodicy seems to look very similar to some forms of social Darwinism (although that is clearly not the intent of those putting forward the G-G theodicy). Simply putting God in charge of the whole thing does not change the morality of it all, only the mechanism by which it is realized. If the argument is that God allows the evil because from it He brings about a greater good, then it is difficult to escape the charge of consequentialism.

Social Justice

I think it is reasonable to ask that, if good comes from evil and the good is necessary, then why stop the evil? In fact, to stop the evil would be to prevent the good. If the good is necessary to the plan of God, then He would need to allow evil in where there will be no interference. Further, if all evil leads to some good not obtainable without the evil, then at what point should God's people obey God's command to stand against evil? As Middleton urges, "Believing the greater good defense would result in nothing less than ethical paralysis."[13] In fact, this might lead to a position suggested by Freidman:

> To be consistent, perhaps the next time we are asked to support famine relief for African children we should simply decline and respond that because the birth rate in the world of nature has already insured the survival of the human species and does not really need these children for its purposes. A morally indifferent universe does not know of moral distinctions, judgements, and designations. There is neither innocence nor evil in such a universe, only events.[14]

Scripture, however, is replete with commands for God's people not to do evil and to prevent it wherever it is found. We are not to permit the weak, the orphan, the widow, the fatherless to be objects of mistreatment (Deut 27:19). In instances where it does happen, God's people are to do everything in their power to stop the evil. In fact, the book of Amos primarily centers on the failure of Samaria to uphold social justice, and God holding them accountable as He holds all accountable for such moral passivity.

Some may argue, however, that God in His wisdom and knowledge uses men through social justice to stop evil that is pointless and this is the good. In this case, two problems arise. One is that this would destroy man's choice to do the good, which makes commands to do good meaningless. If the evil has to be stopped because it will not lead to a good, then in order for it to be certainly stopped, it will have to be determined by God. If it is determined by God, then it is not man's choice to obey—only to do what has been programmed, as an actor on the stage recites the words of another. This would be the only way it could be certain that man would stop the evil, but we have so many cases where man has not stopped the evil. One can think of slavery as an example. So should we then conclude that slavery served God's end purpose to bring good?

The second problem is that the idea of good would be relativized. Under these conditions, it cannot be the particular evil itself about which God is concerned, only that evil as it relates to *that* person in that circumstance (since all social injustice is not prevented by man). If it is not prevented by any means, it must lead to some greater good. So in one place a particular evil might bring forth good, so it would be allowed, and in another place the same evil might be stopped because the stopping of the evil would be the good. The command in the Bible, however, is that social injustice is to always be prevented; that is, it is a universal command. Where God intervenes through His people (or some other means) to prevent social injustice in one place and not in another place (geographical), one can only conclude (if there is no gratuitous evil) that it is not the evil but the individual circumstances that determine God's intervention (either directly or indirectly) in relation to the necessary good. This would seem to make the Scripture's commands to be actively engaged in social justice a relative and not an absolute command.

For those who hold to the openness of God, another difficulty arises. How would God know ahead of time whether the evil would be beneficial since it depends upon the future choices made by man and He cannot know what choices people will make? If God does not know the outcome of the future moral choices of His moral creatures, He cannot possibly know the consequences of those choices; therefore, He will not know which choices to permit and which ones to prevent. In fact, without this knowledge, He might stop a good from coming to pass as well as permit some evil that would not bring about some good.

If certain evil is necessary to certain goods, how will the theist know which evils to permit and which evils to prevent? Whereas under the greater-good justificatory framework the theist cannot always know when the good is achieved (Wykstra's solution), there would not even be a way by which he could design a paradigm on which evils to permit and which ones to try to prevent. Therefore, one would never know if he was preventing an evil or preventing a good. This would convolute the notion of social justice and confuse the definition of good and evil. In one case, *good* is stopping the evil, while in another case, *good* is achieved by permitting the evil. Without charging anyone who holds this position of supporting the idea of *karma*, it does appear that this posture brings one dangerously close to this notion.

What about Prayer?

If, as the G-G theodicy maintains, the only evil permitted by God in this world is that from which He can bring about a greater good or prevent a worse evil, then what about prayer? Suppose a Christian is suffering from cancer. The actuality of cancer, which counts as an evil (physical), means that God has allowed it.

However, God only allows the cancer to bring about a greater good or to prevent a worse evil. Nonetheless, someone brings the name of this person before the church and asks for prayer that God might heal the person from cancer. Here a problem arises.

Why should the church pray that God will stop an evil that He has allowed? Does this not question God's purposes since it is a purposeful (maybe even willed) event? Furthermore, if God answers the prayer of the church, then the initial good He intended never comes and the world is without a necessary good, all because the church prayed. The matter becomes even more difficult if the purpose is to prevent a worse evil. If God answers the prayer of the church and the evil is stopped, then all the church has accomplished is bringing a worse evil upon humanity.

Some might try to answer the question by saying that the evil is God's permissive will, while good health is His perfect will. The question that follows is which will is stronger? It would seem that the permissive will is strongest, which means that His perfect will is subservient. The implications for the eschaton are potentially alarming. When the G-G theodicy is seen in light of prayer, it raises some serious questions for those who believe that prayer is more than a Bingo game and a matter of matching the numbers on earth with the numbers in heaven.

Who Receives the Good?

If one grants that the good obtains, the next logical question is "Good for whom?" According to the principle of "eye for eye, tooth for tooth" (Ex 21:24), the one who suffers is the one to whom the good should accrue. As Eleonore Stump notes:

> It seems to me that a perfectly good entity who was also omniscient and omnipotent must govern evil resulting from the misuse of significant freedom in such a way that the sufferings of any particular person are outweighed by the good which the suffering produces *for that person*; otherwise, we might justifiably expect a good God somehow to prevent that *particular suffering*, either by intervening (in one way or another) to protect the victim, while still allowing the perpetrator his freedom, or by curtailing freedom in some select cases.[15]

Stump's point is well-taken (she is not arguing for gratuitous evil, however), since it is reasonable that the one suffering is the one who should receive the benefit. If there is no gratuitous suffering, there ought to be some evidence that the individual sufferer does in fact benefit from the suffering. In light of this, it is not enough to say that some good somewhere at sometime for someone is reasonable justification for God allowing the evil.

One can think of situations in which it is difficult to argue that a particular evil obtains a good for the individual who is suffering. Consider the case of a man working in the woods by himself. His bulldozer overturns on him. No one hears his cry for help. If he does not get help soon, he will bleed to death. In excruciating pain, the man floats in and out of consciousness. After three hours of agony, he dies, and because he is not a believer, he goes to eternal punishment. It is impossible to see how the good obtains to this man. It seems insufficient to argue, as Swinburne and others do, that from his suffering others learn not to work in the woods by themselves. Here, the most that can be argued is that the good obtains to another and not the one suffering. And further, what if the man had three small children and a wife? Where is the good for them?

There is also the question of horrific and large-scale suffering, such as slavery in the United States or the Holocaust. For whom did the good obtain in these cases? If one argues with Wykstra that the good is beyond our ken, more problems develop. Surely, if an evil of this magnitude is permitted because of some greater good, the good would have to be in proportion to the evil. How could anyone miss this good? Furthermore, if suffering is for the purpose of soul-making, it would be necessary for the good to obtain for the one suffering. So, it is logical that the G-G theodicy maintain that the good does obtain to the ones suffering and not for another.

One might argue that the good obtains to the one suffering, but at a much later point in the sufferer's life—let us say maybe five or ten years later. However, this explanation also raises questions. How can one be sure that the good is in fact directly linked to the suffering from five years ago? Surely there could be many other intervening events in the five-year period which could also account for the state of affairs five years later. Further, how can one be sure that the particular good in question would not have occurred if the suffering had never taken place? How can one be certain that the good is somehow only possible because of a particular suffering event five years previous? It cannot be demonstrated evidentially.

Others argue that the good is God's glory, as suggested by John Piper.[16] However, how is this assessed? It is great to say, but it seems like words uttered without any reference to reality. Now, I am not suggesting that God's glory is not an important consideration for any discussion, much less the questions of evil. But if we claim that the good is that God is glorified, we have to ask ourselves a few further questions. For example, let's take the situation I mentioned earlier of the little girl who was abducted, raped and buried alive. So, we ask, how does this bring glory to God?

Some might say God will get glory when He judges the criminal in the Day of Judgment. But, remember, men go to hell because they are sinners, not because of a particular sin. Particular sins only affirm what God's word says about humanity. So, it is not necessary to have this man brutally violate this little girl and then bury her alive, in order for Him to send this person to hell on the Judgment Day. So, the claim the greater good is for God's glory is a stretch at best and problematic at worst. So, I have a hard time understanding why this particular horrible sin leads to God's glory.

Possibly one could argue that the little girl goes to heaven and that is the good. Let's for a moment accept the view that all children who are not morally accountable go to heaven (a position I am personally willing to embrace). So, you say, the good is that now she is in the Father's care and surely that is good. But, she is not the only one who suffers. What about her mom and dad or siblings, grandparents, etc. I know as a grandparent that if this happened to my granddaughter, I would suffer greatly. So, what is my good since I am suffering? In addition, if it is simply a matter of getting the little girl to heaven, then surely the heavenly, omnipotent, loving Father could find a way that does not involve such horrible means, which by the way, increase the suffering of the loved ones left behind. Of course, Augustine thought that the good was that the death of a child would make better parents. I am not sure how one would make that case to the grieving parents.

In all of this, I think that one of the greatest challenges for theodicy is to have an explanation that satisfactorily deals with the death of little children. We seem to find it easier to accept the death of a bad person or even an old person. While there may be emotional accompaniments with such deaths, it is not with the same questioning heart as when a child is abused and dies. We intuitively sense a protective attitude toward children and are morally incensed when children suffer—whether it is by the hand of a pedophile, a drunken parent, or a horrible disease.

In the end, this question of who gets the good seems to be a very difficult question to answer because especially horrific evils cause so many people to suffer. To say that the good is the glory of God seems thin and weightless indeed, to say nothing of what that says about the kind of God we serve—One who allows one of those whom He loves, created in His image, to suffer horrible deaths just so He can get the glory.

May I add one more concern here, and that is, this position seems to imply that God's glory is not complete without the suffering of his moral beings whom He created. There is something about this whole idea that seems less than theologically sustainable. There may be a good of which I have not thought that would be sufficient grounds to give God moral justification for allowing horrific suffering, but His glory does not seem to be one of them.

Lacks Objective Criteria to Measure Good Against Evil

Another apparent problem for the greater-good premise is the lack of objective criteria for determining when the good outweighs the evil. How is it determined when the good is greater than the evil? How is a value assigned to the act and the consequence even in cases where people think they can see the greater good? As Russell points out in his critique of Hick and Swinburne, "I cannot agree that it [the greater good] is *so* valuable that it could justify someone in permitting suffering like that endured by the little girl in Flint."[17] How does one calculate how much good is needed to make the evil justified? Or, is it just an arbitrary notion subject to anyone's interpretation? The notion of *greater* implies either a quantitative or qualitative measure that requires some means of measurement.

When a measurement is affixed to the discussion, one is faced with a less than desirable conclusion. Consider working from some sort of a numerical value system by assigning a numerical value to suffering, and the same with a good. Let's assign the value of -4 to being beaten (a negative value because it is evil) and the value of +5 to reflect the consequential greater good (a positive value because it is good), and assume that the greater good is obtained. In this case, the net value gain of +1 indicates that the good obtains, which is the basic premise of the G-G theodicy, namely that a greater good obtains.

Consider a second case: in addition to being beaten, a person is also raped and then dismembered while alive. We can assume this evil is worse because it involves additional suffering (assuming that the beating was of equal force in each case). For this suffering we will assign the value of -7 because it is a worse evil and it involves more suffering. In order to represent the obtaining of a greater good, the prevailing good will be assigned a value of +8.

In both cases, we have assigned proportionate positive value to represent the greater good obtains from each respective evil. Both the -4 and the -7 represent real evil events as the +5 and +8 represent real goods. This means that the good obtained in the first case is not of the same magnitude as the good obtained in the second case, or there is a greater good in the second case than in the first. This means that the good obtaining from being beaten and raped is greater (+8) than only being beaten (+5). Logically, it follows that it is better to be beaten and raped than only beaten since the good is greater (something no one actually believes).

Some may object to this example by pointing out that the net gain is the same. This misses the point. Remember that the numerical value for increased good has to be moved up to save the greater-good approach. Unless this move is totally arbitrary, there must be some justification for increasing the numerical value to +8. The only justification is if the actual good increases. Surely a good of the value +8 is better than +5, which is to say the world is better with +8 goods than with only +5 goods. This illustrates the fact that the concept of good in the greater-good approach is neither objective nor constant, and therefore less than meaningful. There is no way to determine what kind of good outranks a particular evil or how much good is needed in order for the greater good to obtain. There is no divine equation to use in order to know what good (or how much good of a particular type) must obtain in order for it to be greater than the corollary evil.

Fails to Answer Mental Attitude Evil

Arthur Flemming also raises another question, which appears to have some force against the greater-good premise. This one addresses the issue of evil that has no actual or overt consequence. A case in point would be where an evil is only *thought,* and not actually committed. This seems to leave some evil outside the explanation of the greater-good approach. Jesus taught that to lust after a woman was to commit adultery (Matt 5:28). As Flemming suggests, "Attempted theft or assault or murder is an evil in itself, but each becomes worse if the attempt succeeds."[18] From a theistic perspective, the thought can also be evil even though it does not become as bad as it might have been if acted upon. Consider the evils of hate, envy and the like, which may never manifest themselves in a way that causes suffering. How is it that good ever comes from such mental attitudes?

It Limits God

I have not said much about the idea that this is the best of all possible worlds, but that discussion is common when dealing with theodicies. Later, I will make my argument that this is the best of all possible worlds, but for now I will simply say that I hold to this position because I believe that when God acts, He must always act according to His perfect being. Geisler and Corduan develop the idea that this is not the best of all possible worlds, but rather the way to the best of all possible worlds. That is, through sin and subsequent redemption, God is able to bring about a better world for humanity—in general terms. While denying that this is the best of all possible worlds, they claim that "this kind of world with free beings who do sin is the best of all possible ways of obtaining the best of all possible worlds, and that no other world or nonworld would have been morally better than this world."[19] The present world is the best it can be under the circumstances, but the circumstances are far from the best. The good achieved by evil will result in a better state for redeemed mankind.

These two authors concede that this is the best world under the circumstances, which includes the fact that man really has freedom. For them, "The actual amount of evil in the world must be the upper limit. If the evil in this world is the necessary condition for bringing about the best of all possible worlds, then we must be experiencing the maximal amount of evil necessary."[20] This sounds a little like the "Let's sin-more-that-grace-may-abound" approach. However, this middle-of-the-road approach comes under the same criticism as other G-G theodicies.

Geisler and Corduan claim that "God must do his best."[21] I agree with this point, that a world with moral beings is a better world than a world without moral beings. Stated in a fuller way, they say, "God must do his best or else it is evil for him. Hence, if God produced anything less than a world that could be produced by an absolutely perfect Being, then God is not an absolutely perfect Being."[22] Their argument runs like this:

1. God is an absolutely perfect Being.

2. Producing less than the best possible world would be an evil for an absolutely perfect Being.

3. But an absolutely perfect Being cannot produce evil.

4. God produced this world.

5. But this world as is and as has been is not the best possible world.

6. Therefore, there must be a perfect world to come (of which this present world is a necessary prelude to its production).[23]

The *best* for Geisler and Corduan is in the eschatological sense, which requires evil as a means of bringing about the best world in the future.

In the end, they argue, that "it is impossible for God to create directly a world with achieved moral values of the highest nature. He must first allow evil as a precondition of the greatest good. Hence, this world with freedom and evil is the best way to produce the morally best possible world."[24] They argue that this world with sin is necessary to the world to come (the Kingdom seems to be that of which they are speaking). God could not have created the best world without a world with evil in it as a necessary precondition to the best world, one with no evil. In the end, God did His best in initial creation, which was not really the best but the best He could do at the time. I am not suggesting that the age to come will not be different in many respects from the age we now occupy, only that that age to come will not be qualitatively intrinsically better than the world as it came from the hand of God recorded in the opening chapters of Genesis.

It does not matter how one defines *best* or *good* in this present argument. It is enough to know that the greater good comes from evil and there is a world (the one to come) where there is no evil. This seems to hold God hostage to evil in order to have the good God knows is best for man, but God is unable to create it apart from using evil. If this is the case, then God is not omnipotent in His creative powers. Note, I am not denying that God can bring good out of evil. I am sure He has, does, and will so long as the present human history continues. What I am saying is that is not the grounds on which He is morally justified in allowing the evil. I must continue to make the point that what God may do with evil does not lay grounds for why he allowed the evil. Please note that these are two different (possibly related issues) questions. To confuse the two is to commit a fallacy that will subvert any theodicy that follows.

CONCLUSION

If the above analysis is correct, then it appears that all traditional G-G theodicies are in need of recasting. Although in the next chapter I will offer a different approach, constructed on a different assumption, it is possible there is some way to redeem the greater good response, but if that is to be the case, it will have to address honestly the objections raised in this chapter. Remember, the purpose of theodicy is not to explain what God might do with evil, but rather on what grounds He is morally justified in permitting evil to continue. While I agree that the cross of Christ is the final word on evil, once again, that is only about how God deals with evil, not why He is presently allowing it. So, for Christians, this is a wonderful message of comfort, but it does not go to the heart of the question raised by the skeptic.

It would seem that the basic assumption or affirmation of the G-G theodicies raises a number of disturbing theological and philosophical concerns. The position that God permits all evil in this world as necessary to the obtaining of some greater good or preventing some greater evil contains difficulties at best and inconsistencies at worst—both within itself and within the larger Christian theological context.

The greater-good premise itself is dubious, and furthermore, requires the denial of gratuitous evil, forcing the theist into the impossible task of demonstrating this from the evidence or from the Bible. In either case, this seems to present itself as a most daunting challenge.

On the strength of what I have said to this point, I would argue that denying gratuitous evil is an unfortunate claim by the theist. In the end, he can only sustain his argument by circular reasoning, which is simply question-begging. The only means of supporting his claim is to assume his conclusion as the basis for making his argument. It is this claim of the greater good (the denial of gratuitous evil) that this author believes is the Achilles heel of the G-G theodicy. Therefore, in the next two chapters we will look at a possible alternative theodicy called the "Creation-Order Theodicy." This will be an attempt to give an alternative response to the question: "God, why this evil?"

NOTES

1. David O'Conner, *God and Inscrutable Evil* (New York: Rowman & Littlefield Publishers, 1998), 1. This book is highly recommended by Daniel Howard-Snyder. In the book, O'Conner interacts with some of the most recent positions on theodicy with a focus on the subject of gratuitous evil. It is a worthwhile book. Even though it may not come down firmly on one side or the other, it does a remarkable job of drawing the lines of distinction within the argument and critiquing several major positions.
2. Stephen John Wykstra, "Rowe's Noseeum Arguments from Evil" in *The Evidential Argument From Evil,* ed. Daniel Howard-Snyder (Bloomington: Indiana University Press, 1996), 127–8.
3. The argument here is not that the claim cannot be made, only that it cannot be made on the strength of the evidence.
4. R. Z. Friedman, "Evil and Moral Agency," *Philosophy of Religion* 24 (1988): 7.
5. Geisler is actually defending against the objection to his position that this is the best way to the best world, but the argument is the same in either case.
6. Norman Geisler, *Philosophy of Religion* (Grand Rapids: Zondervan Publishing House, 1974), 395.
7. Ibid.
8. Friedman, "Evil and Moral Agency," 9.
9. Ibid.
10. Richard J. Middleton, "Why the 'Greater Good' Isn't a Defense," 9 *Koinonia* (1997): 88.
11. Ibid., 91.
12. Friedman, "Evil and Moral Agency," 9.
13. Middleton, "Why 'Greater Good' Isn't a Defense," 91.
14. Friedman, "Evil and Moral Agency," 13.
15. Eleonore Stump, "The Problem of Evil," *Faith and Philosophy* 2 (1985): 411.

16. John Piper, *Spectacular Sins: And Their Global Purpose in the Glory of Christ* (Wheaton: Crossway Books, 2008), 56.
17. Bruce Russell, "The Persistent Problem of Evil," *Faith and Philosophy* 6 (April 1989): 26.
18. Arthur Flemming, "Omnibenevolence and Evil," *Ethics* 26 (January 1986): 270.
19. Geisler and Corduan, *Philosophy of Religion*, 371.
20. Ibid., 378.
21. Ibid., 311.
22. Ibid., 312.
23. Ibid., 343.
24. Ibid., 353.

5
WORLDVIEW CONCEPTS AND THEODICY

When answering the question about the existence of evil in God's creation, the question is really about why God allowed a particular evil. For example, we ponder why God allowed the little girl to be raped and buried alive. Of course, there are always explanations or reasons for evils as they do not happen chaotically. Given choices made by humans, we can always explain evil in terms of cause and effect, but that is not the question here. The "why" question goes to the point of a theodicy, namely, why God allows evil, and particularly evil that is so horrific. As is so often the case with us mortals, we tend to focus very narrowly and selfishly when asking questions such as this. However, that approach usually produces very unsatisfactory answers. Life is complex as well as complicated, and an understanding of the particulars requires a broader understanding of the whole.

You will remember that Michael Peterson has suggested we should approach the work of a theodicy from a worldview perspective. This chapter is dedicated to precisely that, by explaining worldview concepts which will provide the foundation for the proposed theodicy beginning with Genesis one, hence the name *A Creation-Order Theodicy* (C-O). In this chapter I will discuss worldview concepts that impinge upon any theodicy. There are many theological matters I will not address in this chapter as my main concern is to provide a foundation for a main point of this book, namely that gratuitous evil is real but does not count against the moral perfection of God.

Having stated that, the first point I will make is that the existence of God is not a question of personal opinion or preference as it deals with a matter of reality. Either God exists or He does not exist, and the affirmation of either constitutes a philosophical affirmation rather than a religious affirmation. The statement affirms something about the state of affairs referred to as *reality*. God is either there or He is not. It is the same as an affirmation about the existence of tigers. Either tigers exist or they do not exist. Depending on where you are living, your belief about their existence could make a measurable difference. If they do exist, a statement affirming their existence would be a true statement; whereas, denying their existence would be a false statement.

Simply preferring God to exist has no place in the argument. When considering the question of God's existence it must be clear that the force of this question deals with the fact of reality and not one's preference (religious or otherwise) regarding His existence. What must not be lost in the discussion is that what is at stake is one's view of reality. Reality is what it is and either our perception of it is correct or incorrect. Moreover, if God does not exist, then all that has been constructed on the notion that He does exist must be discarded immediately as it would have no value for living in reality. Further, all reasons ever held as good and sufficient to warrant belief in God's existence must be rejected as fool's gold. On the other hand, if God does exist, then what one does with that fact is extremely important.

I will begin with this affirmation: God exists and exists as the personal God of the Bible. This is not merely a statement rooted in wishful thinking, but I make this statement because I believe the evidence for God's existence is compelling. I also affirm that evil exists. Furthermore, it seems rather evident that God and evil stand on opposite sides of things, but the question is whether the reality of evil cancels out the reality of God. From the Christian perspective God and evil both exist, but exist in different ways. God exists as a necessary being, while evil exists only because God created something (He did not create evil). In the end, God deals evil a final blow through Christ's death, burial and resurrection. But remember, that does not answer the question of theodicy. The question of theodicy is why God allows evil to ravage His creation now.

The *Why?* question does not mean that I doubt God as has been pointed out earlier. I do not ask the question because I doubt, but quite the contrary, because I believe. I ask the question of God, not because I think I have found God to be guilty of moral lapse in permitting evil to persist, but precisely because I believe there are answers—answers consistent with everything else I believe about God. Furthermore, I believe God would have us ask of Him how it is that in His divine economy are we to understand the presence of evil in His creation when it is so contrary to His own being. So, I trust I will not suffer the charge of a rationalistic doubter.

HELPFUL CLARIFICATIONS

I think it will be helpful to give three points of clarification. First, it is important to distinguish between affirming one's belief *that* God exists and belief *in* God as a personal religious commitment. The assertion that God exists carries with it no explicit religious connotation. A person can affirm belief *that* God exists without confessing any personal commitment to that God. On the other hand, if a person confesses that he believes *in* God, then something quite different is being said. The first statement conveys what a person thinks about the nature of reality,[1] while the second reveals some personal commitment to God, which is clearly a religious statement. Of course, the second statement would reasonably be made only by one who also affirms the first. It is often the case that the two notions are confused.

It should be pointed out that any affirmation about personal commitments by itself says little or nothing substantively about the existence of God in terms of reality. It is quite possible for God not to exist even though people make some religious commitment to the idea of God. In fact, nothing of epistemological substance is gained for the larger question of God's existence just because someone says he believes in God. Numerous examples abound of religious testimonies affirming notions that are contrary to reality, yet people are very committed to them. Saying that one believes something exists does not say anything substantively about reality. One must examine the reasons why a person believes this or that concerning reality.

Second, one must be clear on what is meant by the affirmation that God limits Himself. It cannot mean that God limits Himself in terms of limiting His essence (who He is). Of course, that would be impossible. How could God in His omnipotence limit His omnipotence so it was no more omnipotence? Pretty impossible I think, as you can see. Rather, the intent of the statement is that God, the Person (whether God the Father, God the Son, or God the Holy Spirit), might limit the *expression* of His essence under certain circumstances in His dealing with humanity within the space/time context.

This can be seen in the Incarnation, in which the second member of the Trinity limits the expression of His attributes (Phil 2:5–8) that He might successfully live among men. In the Incarnation, Jesus was fully God (Heb 1:1–4), yet He limited the expression or appropriation of His divinity to certain circumstances of life. Any possible limited expression of God's nature, however, must not be limited in such a way or to such an extent that it would result in a distorted view of God or entailing a contradiction of who God is in His essence. So, John claims that the disciples "beheld His glory, the glory as of the only begotten of the Father full of grace and truth" (Jn 1:14).

WORLDVIEW CONCEPTS

The argument before us is that the existence of evil makes it more likely that the God of the Bible does not exist than He does exist. Whereas it is the God of the Bible that is in question, it is only reasonable to defend the God of theism in a Christian theodicy.[2] Furthermore, the atheist must use the Bible to get his idea of God; likewise, it seems legitimate to use the Bible in defending God in this context. The atheist cannot use the Bible to construct the objection and then deny the theist the same right to consult the Bible. If the whole argument against God comes from an understanding of God as presented in the Bible, then to be consistent, one cannot deny the use of the Bible in the defense when it speaks to the matter of God. I would want to emphasize, however, that though I believe God is more than the omnipotent, omniscient, wholly good, personal being, He is not *less*. In this book I have focused on the three attributes because those are precisely the attributes used to criticize the belief that this kind of God exists in light of evil.

The Nature of God and Creation

Evil exists because God created something good. Evil cannot exist by itself as it has no essence of its own (Augustine). Evil is a lack in that which is good. In this sense, evil is not a thing, but rather a condition of privation in something that is good.[3] Here I am not saying that particular acts of evil are merely a privation in something; what I am saying is that the condition of what we call *evil* is like a virus or corruption in God's creation. We might say the principle of corruption has touched every good thing in God's creation. This corruption is manifest by particular acts that pound relentlessly upon all aspects of creation.

Prior to any act of creation (angels, man, and the universe) there was only God. Furthermore, since all that existed eternally is God (who is absolute), whatever He created had only His nature (absolute goodness) to guide the process and His mind to design the product. Consequently, one cannot separate the nature of God from the nature of what was created. This is not to say that the nature of God and creation are identical, only that whatever God created reflects His perfect character—for no other pattern existed. This, however, is not to imply that creation was perfect in the same way that God is perfect. That would be impossible as God is uncreated and immaterial, while the world is created and material. By virtue of its created*ness* it cannot be uncreated*ness*.

I assume there is little debate on the point that there is an essential difference between *created* and *uncreated*. Nonetheless, what God created was controlled and informed only by His perfect nature, for there was nothing else after which to pattern it –for all there was, was God. This means that within the category of *created*, what God created was perfect to the degree and kind that a created thing can own perfection. It is a logical impossibility for God to create a perfection belonging only to that which is uncreated—His perfection.

Furthermore, had God never created anything, it would be impossible for evil to exist. Another way to say this is that evil is not a created entity, as Augustine and Aquinas both affirmed. In principle, evil is the privation of the good; it is some corruption of the good. There was no flaw in creation that could be called *evil*. This point must not be lost on us as the importance rests in the fact that God is not the author nor creator of evil. Everything in the Garden was very good (Gen 1:31) and that included the tree of the knowledge of good and evil. I will say more about this later. I want to remind you what I am doing so you do not become discouraged in trying to follow all of this. Remember, I am trying to build a worldview context within which we understand the problem of evil in order to construct a theodicy that does not suffer the same weaknesses as the G-G theodicies.

God and Man

I will argue that it is also the proper place to begin the work of theodicy as in the early chapters of Genesis. It is there that God provides information on the basic *modus vivendi* (a feasible arrangement that circumvents difficulties) to which He voluntarily commits in order to establish a predictable and meaningful relationship with man. Just as it is necessary to understand the rules by which a game is played beforehand, so it is necessary to understand under what terms and conditions God establishes for the mutual interaction between Himself and man. Imagine watching a baseball game and the batter hits the ball and runs successfully to first base. However, an infielder on the other team stops the ball and throws it to first base, whereupon the umpire tells the runner that he is out—he is no longer allowed to stay on first base. Now, if you are watching the game but have no awareness of the rules of the game, you might think that this is unfair. After all, the batter did hit the ball and he did run to first base. What makes the difference regarding how you view the events that follow is that you know the rules of the game. So it is with creation.

God has established certain terms and conditions (the rules of creation order) that establish how the infinite personal God can meaningfully and predictably interact with finite personal man. God, who is eternal (without a past from which He came, or a future into which He will become), is on a different order than man, who is a created being, and it is the rules of creation that make the relationship between man and God possible. Prior to the existence of matter, the triune God existed in social harmony as Trinity. Within this trinitarian complex the Father, the Son and the Holy Spirit enjoy a perfect relationship with one another. Jesus expressed something of this relationship when He was here on earth. As He prayed to the Father the night of His betrayal, He spoke of the glory which He had with the Father "before the world was" (Jn 17:5). The question after creation is how the infinite and the finite could have a meaningful personal relationship. I want to stress the idea of *personal* (I do not mean private possession, but person-to-person relationship).

When God (the Trinity) acts through and towards those within the Divine community, the essence of God is unrestricted in manifestation. Therefore, one can speak of the Divine persons acting/interacting without restriction within the Trinity. The second condition in which the personal God acts/interacts involves that which is outside His essence and person, namely the circle of created reality.

While there is compatibility between God and man, they do not share the same order, as one is created and the other is not. God by sovereign choice created man as a personal moral being, which suggests that God intended to interact relationally (I mean by that, that God would interact with man as a true person), with man in *similar* fashion to His relation within the Trinity. Whereas God is sovereign, He alone determines the manner by which He interacts in a person-to-person relationship. This makes possible a meaningful relationship even though His moral beings are created creatures and He is not. In order for this relationship to be authentic, it requires some limitation of the expression of some of God's attributes. This is so because no man has ever seen God directly and lived (Jn 1:18). Man only saw God in Christ as veiled in flesh (Heb 10:20) — a limited expression of divinity.

What we must grasp first is that God limits the expression of Himself (His God*ness* or essence) in the interest of establishing a meaningful person-to-person relationship with man. Anything else requires God to be always at such a distance from man that that distance would inhibit a meaningful relationship with man. This is hinted at in Deuteronomy 5:23–27; 18:15–19. Within the Trinity the relationship is among equals and grounded in the eternal perfect moral character of each of the three persons in the Godhead. Whereas the created realm does not possess that same perfection, God's personal interaction with created personal beings must have a special *modus vivendi* which takes into account the limitations and creaturely possibilities of created persons.

It is this *modus vivendi* that makes it possible for two persons of different ontological order (status) to have a meaningful relationship in which the relationship is volitional and not determinative or coercive. This is another most important fact to remember. Do not forget, the greatest commandment is that we love God (Mat 22:37–40). Love requires a real freedom, which means responsibility as freedom requires the uninhibited reality of choice. It is this choice that I have referred to as *libertarian freedom* in earlier chapters.

Whereas man is made in the image of God, he has a mind. The mind is essential to the possibility of choice as it is with the mind that we understand choices and make judgments between possibilities. With this mind man is capable of intentionally loving both God (which includes obeying God) and other created moral beings (at least moral beings; I am not qualified to say what exists between a man and his dog). With the actualization of creation, two minds (that is, two kinds of minds—an uncreated mind and created mind) now exist in reality—the mind of God and the mind of man. God's mind operates on the infinite level and man's operates on a finite level—and yet there is meaningful intersection of and interaction between the two within creation order.

The *modus vivendi* we will call "creation order" is what establishes the moral and physical parameters (terms and conditions) by which God is able to have a meaningful person-to-person relationship with mankind. Creation order is the context within which it is possible for man and God to have a meaningful relationship. It is also what makes possible God's sustaining relationship with creation in general (Col 1:17).

On same grounds, this is what makes it possible for man to respond volitionally to this God in love (an important point noted by Hick). Whatever moral and physical parameters God establishes issue forth from His eternal, sovereign, all-wise, just and loving essence, and from the point of creation forward would be binding on both God the person and on man in any relationship that would exist between the two. The creation order would be just for all concerned and would make it possible for man to be a real person in the same way that God is a real person. Furthermore, this order was constructed in such a way that the providence of God assures the fulfillment of the counsels of God (Is 45–47), while at the same time giving man libertarian freedom. By this, man in some sense has influence on the shape of history through his choices, although those choices never cancel out the counsels of God.

Two Minds

Man, who is made in the image (shadow image) of God, appears to be the most complex and unique part of creation (Gen 1:26–27). Part of what constitutes the image of God in man is that man is a moral being with a mind capable of moral judgment (a point made by Leibniz). In this way, man is not only an expression of the mind of God, but is given a mind patterned after God's mind. This means that at least some of the same categories of thought in the mind of God are also in the mind of man. Because of this, the mind of man is capable of comprehending God's thoughts as those thoughts have been revealed by God to man in the Bible (1 Cor 2:16). It also means that the world in which man lives is intelligible to man because God created both the world and the mind of man, so there is a correspondence between the categories in the mind of man and the structure of reality.

The human mind must not be thought of as simply a repository for data. It is much more than that. The human mind has the capacity of rational cognition by which information is processed and utilized in various ways. It is because of this that God can reveal His mind to man in the Bible, which is a book that can guide man (Ps 119:105). This Word is not magical or mystical; it has been given for our understanding and application to life. Furthermore, once the mind comprehends the Word, the will moves the mind to respond to information in either a positive or negative way (the early Augustine).

Man's mind is not controlled by some divinely created software that determines how the information will be appropriated as that would not be a real mind, it would be a machine. The mind has the capability of processing the information correctly or rejecting it out of hand.[4] If the mind were wired to love God in a predetermined fashion, it would be impossible for man not to love God. How God wired the mind would determine how man would act, in which case man would have no responsibility in the matter. If the wiring of the man meant that man could not love God, then the command to love God would be cruel. What is argued here is that essential to being morally free is the freedom to actually accept or reject information, to choose to do something or to refrain from doing it. We see this very process in the first chapter of Romans where it says that man chooses to reject what he sees in nature that points to God (Ro 1:18–19).

It appears from the Genesis account of creation that God truly desired to have another mind outside Himself as part of the universe. This would be a mind with which He could share in a personal way and establish a reciprocating loving relationship. Without libertarian freedom[5] (I actually prefer the term Thomas Flint calls *libertarian traditionalism*)[6] love is impossible, since by definition love is a volitional matter that requires judgment, either to love or not to love. This is what I will call an *authentic mind,* and it includes the capacity for judgment. By *judgment* I mean the ability to assess information, consider alternatives, form predictions, and consider possible outcomes or consequences in advance of any choice. Raw information (data) without judgment is what one may have in a computerized machine, but the human mind is different.

For example, one can control a rocket by programming it a certain way, but in this case, the machine has no power of judgment. In fact, one can even program it to function differently when it detects different conditions, but that is all according to the programming. This is not judgment of mind—it is control. One cannot command a machine, only control it. Of course, it is technically possible to command a machine through voice-recognition programs, but the machine's response is still limited according to its program. Its response might look like human judgment, but it only has similarity, not sameness. The Bible gives commands and then assigns penalties when the commands are disobeyed (example: Deut 28–30). Furthermore, it is clear that there are limits to what the human mind can choose. I suggest that creation order limits the choices available from which the human mind can choose. These outer limits provide a moral framework so that the human mind can operate as an authentic mind influencing history, but do so without overriding or canceling out the cosmic plan of God.

While it is true that the mind of man and the mind of God function on different levels, there is an intersection at the existential level. God is able to give man instructions about his relationship to and responsibility for creation (Gen 2:15–17 and 2:19 in the naming of the animals). It is amazing that God gives man the task of naming the animals. They are the creation of God and so known to God. However, they could also be known to man so that his naming served the true purposes of God—he was actually able to name them properly. We must not understate the significance of this event. Likewise, the mind of man is able to comprehend the mind of God in revealed matters, but is free to either obey or disobey

It is also possible for God to give man moral instruction in such a way that the mind of God accurately communicates to the mind of man and man is morally responsible (Gen 2:17). Failure to follow God's moral instruction can result in serious moral/physical consequences for man even as God instructs (Gen 3:1–19). When Adam is confronted with his disobedience, he does not offer a defense based on not understanding what God had said (Gen 3:10–12). He clearly understood the speech of God before the Fall as well as after the Fall. It is instructive to note that God has a face-to-face discourse with man after man has died spiritually. Furthermore, even in a fallen state, man was able to comprehend what God was saying. I believe this has something very significant to say to us about how the unsaved person operates in this world in relation to knowledge of God from different sources as well as how this shapes history.

The two minds work in conjunction with one another and are responsible for the shape of human history within the creation order. Man's mind contributes to the content of history, but always within limits of the ultimate plan of God.[7] In some sense, as Udo Middelmann explains, "There is an openness to history, a realization that life is not following tracks set in concrete."[8] This is not to be confused with open theism. I am not saying, nor is Middelmann, that God does not know the future, but only that our choices in life do make a difference. Our lives are not the result of a predetermined cause and effect where we are merely playing out the tune divinely inscribed upon our minds from the beginning. God's knowledge of the future choices of his moral agents is not necessarily causal knowledge—He simply knows it.

Regardless how far man may go against God, man's actions can never go too far for two reasons. First, he is limited in what he can do by virtue of the moral ordering itself. This means that when man attempts to live against the moral structure of the universe, God will providentially intervene with appropriate action. Second, man is limited by intrinsic physical and mental limitations—he is finite in all respects. However, as is seen in Genesis 11:1–9, even in a fallen state (which includes man's mind), man's mind is capable of some rather amazing feats. It also reveals how the providence of God limits in certain ways man's plans. These parameters establish how the will of God and the will of man function together within the matrix of God's creation order. I am reminded of Mrs. Whatsit's explanation of form and freedom to Calvin. She uses the idea of the sonnet. She says:

> "And each line has to end with a rigid rhyme pattern. And if the poet does not do it exactly this way, it is not a sonnet, is it?"
> "No."
> "But within this strict form the poet has complete freedom to say whatever he wants, doesn't he?"
> "Yes." Calvin nodded again.
> "So," Mrs. Whatsit said.
> "So what?"
> "Oh, do not be stupid, boy!" Mrs. Whatsit scolded. "You know perfectly well what I am driving at!"
> "You mean you're comparing our lives to a sonnet? A strict form, but freedom within it?"
> "Yes." Mrs. Whatsit said. "You're given the form, but you have to write the sonnet yourself. What you say is completely up to you."[9]

I would suggest this illustrates the relationship between human libertarian freedom and the structure of God's creation order. Creation order determines the parameters within which man exercises the legitimate use of his libertarian freedom.[10] In order for the two minds to interact within a context of community, freedom must exist for both parties. If man is to love God, then he must be free to respond to the person of God. As Hick notes, love cannot be coerced as this would not be love. Jesus taught that the two great commandments concern love—love for God and man—and on these two laws hang everything else (Matt 22:37–40). Whatever happened to the mind in the Fall does not mean that the mind ceased to be a mind capable of loving and knowing as well as capable of choosing between legitimate options.

Something is learned of the relationship between the mind of God and the mind of man by considering the Incarnation. Here one sees what was truly intended for man. For example, Jesus (God-man) prays to the Father: not my will, but your will be done (Matt 26:39, 42). In addition, Scripture speaks of Jesus doing the will of the Father which pleases the Father (Matt 17:5), and Jesus says He does not do His own will, but the will of the Father who sent Him (Jn 5:30, 6:38). Here one sees how the two minds were intended to work together—the human voluntarily (freely) submitting to the divine in matters where the divine has made His mind clear.

Unless this is just a piece of theater where words are spoken for the audience and nothing more, this must be taken seriously as representative of the optimum relationship between the divine and human mind—the divine and human will. Jesus, the man, submitted to the creation order while here on earth. He exhibited that, while there is a difference between the divine mind and the human mind, there need be no conflict.

Moral Ordering of Contingent Reality

The command regarding the tree of knowledge of good and evil (Gen 2:17) demonstrates that man was given a choice and that the direction of human history would be influenced by the choice made. It seems clear that if man does not eat, he will live and if he eats, he will die. That is a real difference, a difference so great that the second person of the Trinity comes into the world to remedy what happened in the Garden. The question that stands before us is why man chooses to act contrary to the command of God if the mind of man is created by God. Surely, the will itself could not be evil, for as Augustine, Aquinas, and Leibniz argued, the will itself is good because it comes from God. The answer is found in Augustine's response to this question. The will has the power to turn in an inappropriate direction to do what is against the divine moral command as well as the power to turn after the proper and the good.

It seems that Leibniz is correct when he concludes that the answer is found in the reality of creation. For Leibniz, the weakness is in the "ideal" nature of man. He writes, "We must consider that there is an *original imperfection in the creature* before sin, because the creature is limited in his essence; whence ensues that it cannot know all, and that it can deceive itself and commit other errors."[11] The nature of man, although it is morally good (in fact, the best a created moral being could be), is limited by the fact it is created (finite), which means man is finite in every respect, including knowledge. Therefore, it is impossible for man, as a creature, to know everything. The limitedness (man as a finite creature) of man's "ideal" nature (his nature was good because it came from God) proves to be the opportunity for evil. It is not a moral defect or deficiency, but rather an ontological limitedness necessary to man's creatureliness.

Adam, in his attempt to overcome his limitedness, chose to not love God, and disobeyed God in an attempt to be like God (unlimited). God had warned that should that happen, death would come upon creation. From this flows (either directly or indirectly) all suffering and pain in this world. This is the result of man's choice to not love God and to act in self-interest, leaving all creation (including man) corrupted and in some sense distanced from God. It is the inappropriate use of the will that brings evil, not God. God is not morally responsible for the limitation in man, for all created beings of necessity have this limitation. Anything created could not be limitless in all or any respects, for such an attribute belongs only to God who is uncreated. Libertarian freedom is what is necessary for man to love God and to live properly within creation. Creation order is what places the boundaries on this freedom so as to secure the cosmic plan of God. The consequences of man's rebellion and misuse of his freedom, although it was very severe, did not go beyond the bounds of God's knowledge, nor did it in any way change the counsels of God for humanity. In the Kingdom, redemption through Christ will restore redeemed humanity to its place in God's creation as intended in Genesis two.

Ordering Nature

It seems there can be little doubt that there is an ordering of the physical operation of what has been created. The facts of the universe with its regularity and predictability are learned early in school science classes. In practical terms, this physical ordering is binding upon all who wish to live safely in the universe or who wish to harness the powers of nature for human use. For example, anyone desiring to build an airplane must abide by the laws of physics. This ordering limits what man can do, or at least the way in which he does it. It includes the principle of cause and effect. The physical ordering, however, is not ultimately what maintains the universe in its orderly fashion. It is simply the framework within which God works in the space/time context.

The Bible teaches that Christ holds all things together (Col 1:17; Heb1:3) and He is faithful to His creation (1 Pet 4:19). As such there is a certain observable regularity within creation order (Gen 8:22). This makes science possible. What is witnessed by man as regularity in the universe is the result of Christ's faithfulness to natural order. However, this regularity is not the final word in nature; Christ is. So when speaking of the creation order, this does not present a picture of a deistic God.[12] Miracles are compatible within the physical ordering of creation as all is in submission to the providence of God. God can intervene in the physical order as long as in doing so He neither contradicts His own character nor inflicts harm unjustly to His moral beings.

While physical ordering of the universe seems without debate, the idea of a moral ordering in the universe is not so readily accepted. I suggest, however, that the moral ordering is equally true of our universe. The fact is, all of humanity thinks in moral categories, which is not to say that everybody agrees on what belongs to each category, but they do agree on the categories—good and bad, right and wrong are examples. The Ten Commandments (Ex 20) express something of the moral ordering. In Romans 2:1–16 we learn that all men think and act in moral categories. This is the way, at least, our planet is structured, and that structure is part of the way man is. His humanness reveals the reality of this structure, which is a reflection of the structure of reality itself. It is this moral structure that explains why matters go bad when man acts against this structure, just as it happens when man goes against the physical structure of his world. If one violates the moral structure, there are consequences, and sometimes, very dire consequences. When someone like Hitler goes against the moral structure, there is great evil, even gratuitous evil I would say. It is not God doing something; it is man acting against the moral structure. In the next chapter we will see how this plays a part in the theodicy I propose.

Covenant Restrictions

In addition to the moral and physical ordering of creation, God has also limited Himself by certain covenants, which form part of the creation order. For example, in Genesis 3 there is a promise to humanity about redemption (Gen 3:15). In Genesis 9, His covenant with Noah guarantees that the earth would never again be covered by a flood of water (Gen 9:11). Such covenant proclamations were initiated by God and without provocation, as God is sovereign. Once a covenant of this nature is made, God must abide by the terms of the covenant He voluntarily established. There are other such covenants, such as the covenant with Abraham in Genesis 17, assuring the descendants of Abraham a land as well as kings and greatness. Furthermore, in Jeremiah 31, a new covenant binds God to certain activities in relationship to the redeemed. These covenants support the point that beyond the particular creative ordering of the universe, God has also committed to certain covenants He has made with humanity or special groups within humanity. These covenants limit God the person to certain actions, not because He has lost power to do otherwise, but precisely because He is the immutable God. He keeps His self-restricting word, which is primarily for man's benefit. Such covenants contribute to the structure within which libertarian freedom operates while at the same time assuring the end will be as God has promised.

Sovereignty and Prayer

Often the simple definition of *sovereignty* is that God can do whatever He wishes, which is only true if the statement is qualified. There are things that God cannot do, namely things that are logically impossible or contradictory. I think this is rather self-evident, but not all would agree with that assessment. However, beyond this, there are things that the sovereign God cannot do within the space/time context which are self-limiting concerns. As mentioned earlier, God's interaction with His creation is limited by His own sovereign choice. Consider, for example, God has sovereignly chosen to save men only through

Christ. He is not free to save men any other way because He has limited Himself to that way alone. That, however, is not a challenge to His sovereignty. What I am saying is that when God works within creation He is limited in what He can do, by virtue of antecedent sovereign choices to act in a certain way.

To stand in the circle of uncreated reality—God—and say God can do whatever He chooses to do in that strata of reality is logically possible and is a correct statement. To stand, however, in the circle of created reality—creation— and make the same statement is simply not so. These are different existent orders, but not contrary orders as God created the material. It is simply wrong to claim that because God is sovereign that there are no limits to what He can choose to do in time/space. In light of this, there is a relationship between how we pray and what God is free to do in answering those prayers.

First, it should be pointed out that prayer is one aspect of the creation order as it has been established by God's sovereign choice. God has worked into His creation order the principle of prayer by which God will, under certain circumstances, respond to the requests of the righteous man (Ja 5:16). Prayer was constructed so it did not eliminate God's sovereignty, but provided a vehicle for man truly to petition God to act in space/time based upon a prayer, and as a result, affect the shape of history. However, answers to prayers are always within the limits set by the creation order, but they are real answers relative to the human request. Petitionary prayer is more than matching one's request with the predetermined will of God in heaven.

The events surrounding the serious illness of Hezekiah recorded in 2 Kings 20:1–11 provide an instructive lens through which to appreciate the reality of God working in space/time as it relates to prayer. This text illustrates the reality of God responding to a prayer of one of His own and changing the direction of history for that person and beyond. Upon hearing from the prophet Isaiah that he will die, Hezekiah prays to God to grant him more days on earth. God stops Isaiah, who had left before Hezekiah began his prayer, and tells him to return and tell Hezekiah that he will not die in the next day or so. In fact, God says that He will give Hezekiah fifteen more years.

The change came precisely because of Hezekiah's prayer. God says, "I have heard your prayer, I have seen your tears; surely I will heal you" (2 Kg 20:5b). The prophet was right when he first brought the message from God. At that point in space/time the king was going to die, so the message was true. It was true in relation to the point on the space/time continuum when it was spoken. Had the king not prayed, he would have died within the next few days as the true prophet of God had said. Hezekiah, however, did pray, and God answered the precise content of the prayer. When Isaiah returned to the king and told him he was going to live, this was true at that moment of time. So the prophet speaks truth in both cases.

Here is a clear example of prayer changing matters in history, but only within the limits of the creation order as determined by the wise and just God. Such limits give God the freedom to answer a prayer of man and at the same time not abrogate His counsel. This is why we always acknowledge that our prayers are offered realizing there are limits to what God can do, so we say "Your will be done." Furthermore, His providence works in conjunction with the answer to prayer to insure the proper ending of all things.

Persuasion and Human Freedom

Persuasion is another part of the creation order whereby one can influence the mind of another without violating his libertarian freedom. This goes for God as well. God can effectively persuade man without compromising the principle of individual freedom. Persuasion never violates the person even though God may use extreme means to persuade some men. An example of this is the persuasive act of God in the life of Saul of Tarsus (Acts 9:1–4). In the matter of salvation, all men are persuaded sufficiently to repent and trust Christ (Jn16:7–11). However, in many cases this persuasive work of God may be resisted (Acts 7:51; Heb 3:7–11, 15; 4:6, 7). The vehicle of persuasion is one way by which God is able to influence men while respecting the freedom of His moral agents.

Sometimes God persuades through signs. Think of Moses who had a command from God to lead His people out of Egypt. Moses was resistant. God persuades Moses with the miracle of turning a stick into a serpent (Ex 3–4). Gideon is another example. When Gideon is told by the Angel of the Lord to deliver Israel from the hand of Midianites, he questions the task. The miracle of the sacrifice being consumed and the fleece convince him to do as commanded. During His earthly ministry, Jesus responds to those who question His words to believe because of His works (Jn 10:38). These examples illustrate the principle of persuasion whereby God is able to move men to choose or do the right thing under the circumstances without violating their freedom of choice. Not everyone who was the object of God's persuasive acts were in fact persuaded to the right choice. Consider the Exodus generation. They resisted God's Spirit (Heb 3:7–11), so after ten times, God decided to no more try to persuade them (Num 14:20–24).

MIDDLE KNOWLEDGE AND THE BEST OF ALL POSSIBLE WORLDS

This section began by suggesting that when trying to develop a theodicy that it is important to do so from a worldview perspective. That is, we need to know how creation interacts with its creator. I have pointed out several important aspects of what I have called *the creation order*. That is, considering the rules of the game, so to speak. Before God created anything, He decided how He would interact with His creation, and especially how He would interact with the moral being called man. If man is to be a true moral being, then he must have libertarian freedom, but there must be limits to that freedom. It is creation order that provides such limits both on God's activities with man and man's use of his libertarian freedom.

If man is truly free, then that would explain why there is evil in this world, but because there is a limit to man's freedom, the evil does not destroy God's ultimate goal for His creation. There are two other factors I think important to understanding the problem of evil. One is the concept of *middle knowledge*, and the other is the notion of this being the best of all possible worlds. I think middle knowledge is a way to understand how God's sovereignty and the integrity of man's libertarian freedom work together without denying either. I will not defend middle knowledge here; only show how it fits into my understanding of theodicy. The second point is that I will affirm that this is the best of all possible worlds. This I believe is important as it assures the theist that what is could not be improved upon, thereby lessening the need for some greater-good premise.

Middle Knowledge

The idea of middle knowledge seems to be consistent with the teaching of Scripture regarding God's omniscience. Here it is suggested that God's omniscience includes middle knowledge, a view introduced by Spanish Jesuit theologian and philosopher Luis de Molina (1535–1600). According to this view, God's omniscience encompasses three types of knowledge: natural knowledge, free knowledge and middle knowledge. According to Thomas Flint, natural knowledge refers to the necessary truths—those truths innate to God. It is God's natural knowledge that "provides God with knowledge of which worlds are possible."[13] God's natural knowledge encompasses all possibilities. His middle knowledge knows all that would happen under different circumstances and his free knowledge is that He knows all things that will happen. Middle knowledge includes the knowledge God has regarding all the non-determined acts of His moral agents in all possible circumstances.

Further, Flint explains, "Molina's answer is that knowledge of counter-factuals of creaturely freedom is part neither of God's natural knowledge nor of his free knowledge, but instead is part of a third category of knowledge which lies between the other two."[14] When we speak of a counterfactual, think of it as a hypothetical; that is, we might say "If I had gone to college, today I would be making more money." That is a simple example of a counterfactual. We do find such language in the Bible regarding God knowing counterfactuals. For example, in 1 Samuel 13:13–14 we find that God knew that had Saul been faithful, he would have retained his kingdom. In 1 Samuel 23:10–13 God tells David what would happen if he stayed in Keilah. In Matthew 11:12–13, Jesus tells what would have happened in Tyre and Sidon under different circumstances. Kenneth Keathley, after giving several examples from the Bible of counterfactual knowledge, says, "Counterfactual statements are remarkably common (Matt 26:24; Jn 15: 22, 24; 18:26; 1 Cor 2:8; *passim*)."[15]

By His middle knowledge, God knew all the possible worlds, and from the possible worlds chose to actualize the best world of those possible worlds. The perspective supported here is that God's middle knowledge is what made it possible for Him to see conceptually all the free choices of His moral creatures in various possible circumstances and then actualize the best of those possible worlds. At this place, I am not defending middle knowledge; I am accepting it as a legitimate understanding of God's omniscience.[16] I think there are good and sufficient reasons for accepting middle knowledge which is not theological system-sensitive as one can find both Calvinist and non-Calvinist who accept some form of middle knowledge. It is middle knowledge that explains how men have the freedom of choice, while God determines the circumstance within which each choice is made. This understanding supports a robust view of God's providence as well as a libertarian view of man's freedom. My purpose for introducing middle knowledge here is as a way of understanding the concept of "best of all possible worlds."

Best of all Possible (Feasible) Worlds

It would appear that the concept of the best of all possible (feasible) worlds is more understandable if God actually has middle knowledge.[17] It seems, however, a case could be made for the best of all possible worlds without appealing to middle knowledge. Middle knowledge seems more straightforward because God knows that a possible world is best because He knows it in some true sense before He actualizes it. If God has middle knowledge, then He truly knows each world before He actualizes one. Under such conditions, God knows all true counterfactuals which would be true knowledge prior to actualization of any world. As William Craig says:

> Considerations pertinent to divine providence and predestination require that God possess His knowledge of true counterfactuals logically prior to His decree to actualize some world. As for the means of such middle knowledge, God does not derive His knowledge from any predetermination or comprehension of the will, but rather possesses innately an immediate intuition of all truth simply in virtue of His being God.[18]

This understanding of middle knowledge appears to escape the objection related to counterfactuals.

The matter of this being the best of all possible worlds is not without its adversaries. A few object to the notion of possible worlds as philosophically unacceptable on the grounds that it is incoherent. Swinburne believes "it follows that the objection from the existence of God is not that he did not create the 'best of all possible worlds', for to do that is not logically possible: there is no best of all possible worlds."[19] Others such as Alvin Plantinga would say there is no way to know what a best possible world looks like. Bruce R. Reichenbach concludes that "there could be no best possible world, since for any world which we would name there would always be another which was more optimific. Again, the notion of best possible world proves to be meaningless."[20] Alvin Plantinga argues that "no matter how marvelous a world is—containing no matter how many persons enjoying unalloyed bliss—isn't it possible that there be even a better world containing even more persons enjoying even more unalloyed bliss?"[21] Agreeing with Plantinga, Peterson writes, "We now know that it is simply not true that God, if he exists, could have actualized any possible world. Another error in the argument is that it seems to presuppose that there *is* 'a best of all possible worlds,' a concept that is incoherent."[22] I am not convinced that the idea is incoherent if understood from a deductive approach, namely, affirming that this is the best of all possible worlds because God always does what is best. Furthermore, I think the idea is coherent when we understand 'world' to reference all of creation—from the day of creation to the day of final realization of the Kingdom.

Although many have dismissed any idea of a best world as philosophically unacceptable, others think it has possibilities. David Blumenfeld indicates in his discussion of Leibniz's notion that this is the best of all possible worlds (*BPW*). When Leibniz is understood, it follows that his position entails an "implicit proof of the consistency of the concept of the *BPW*."[23] Blumenfeld suggests that it is possible to hold to this possibility without denying God's freedom.[24] Leibniz, however, believed that the character of God requires God to do His best, but not that God has no choice in the matter. Blumenfeld summarizes Leibniz's position as: "Being omnipotent, God could have created any possible world he pleased; but, being all-good, he would certainly have chosen to create the very best world."[25]

Another advocate of the best of possible worlds, David Schrader, claims: "If God is good He will surely create the best of all possible worlds."[26] In a helpful article, R.W. K. Paterson defines what he understands by the notion that God is perfectly good: "I shall take this to mean that God chooses to create the best world that is logically capable of being created, 'the best of all possible worlds'."[27] C. Mason Myers maintains that "[o]n the other hand a deity having omnipotence, omniscience, and omni-benevolence as necessary attributes must of *necessity* create a world of maximum possible goodness if he is to create at all," which for Myers is the "best of all possible worlds."[28]

What is in view here when speaking about a *best world* is its moral integrity, not the felicity of the inhabitants of such a world. I think Philip Quinn makes one of the strongest points for this being the best of all possible worlds. He notes that "If an omnipotent and superlatively good moral agent had to choose between less than complete felicity and surpassable moral goodness when actualizing a possible world, he would choose less than complete felicity."[29] The point Quinn makes is that it matters what one uses to judge whether or not this is the best of all possible worlds. Is it felicity or moral integrity? I think on that count, moral integrity wins the day. I think that both on philosophical as well as theological terms that it is reasonable to conclude that this is the best of all possible worlds, when *world* is understood as the complete book from creation to the final realization of the Kingdom.

At the core of my justification for the claim that this is the best of all possible worlds is the understanding of what the word *world* signifies. The word *world* primarily refers to the realm of humanity and its culture (See Jn 3:16; 2 Tim 4:10; 1 Jn 2:15). Therefore, it includes humanity from the point of creation to the full realization of the Kingdom of God on this earth forever. *World* does not refer to any particular periodic arrangement under which man lives. It is as Leibniz confesses, "I call 'World' the whole succession and the whole agglomeration of all existent things . . . For they must needs [*sic*] be reckoned all together as one world, or, if you will, as one Universe."[30] Biblically, it appears there are different stages or states of affairs (ages) as a part of this world's history, but there is only one "world" that exists from the point of creation (Mk 10:30; Lk 20:34; 2 Cor 4:4). There have been changes to this world (such as what happened in the Fall), but this does not constitute another world, nor does the Kingdom to come (or heaven) constitute another world. There is real continuity from creation to the Kingdom (or whatever one understands the final form this world will assume). Those who will populate the Kingdom belong to this world and not another as brought into being, as recorded in Genesis 1.

Christ came to redeem this world and not another. Therefore, when affirming that this is the best of all possible worlds, we are not looking at some particular state of affairs at any one point, but the whole. For example, surely one can think of things being a little better than what they are at the particular moment, but this is not what is meant when it is affirmed that this is the best of all possible worlds. Moreover, to call heaven or the Kingdom of God another world seems philosophically unacceptable as a possible world because it would break continuity with this world. Christ came not to create another world, but to redeem this world.

Of course, one regularly hears people say that God created this world and when people (not the Bible, as the Bible says God created the heavens and the earth and all that is therein—Exodus 20:11) use the word "world," they are referring to the material creation. There is no sense in the Bible where *create* is used of human history. The statement that God actualized this world refers to the history of humanity as well as the material aspect of creation. To say that God created the history of this world would mean that the entire human history is determined. The distinction seems obvious as well as necessary. If God created the history of the cosmos, then there really is no discussion at all, as the history of the cosmos would simply be a piece of theater with players following a predetermined *possible* that carries two important notions.

The first is that there are some worlds that are simply not possible (that is, not feasible). Here the word implies limitations on what worlds could actually exist. One world that is impossible or unfeasible is a world where all free men obey and love God. In a second way, *possible* signals the fact there are limitations on anything that is created. In this way the term *possible* means that this world is the best it can be given the fact that it is created. In that it is created, it cannot have the moral perfection as experienced by God. So, there are some limitations to what *possible* can include when applied to the quality of that which is created. To say that this is the best of all possible worlds entails that there are some worlds not possible and that, of the possible worlds, there are limits to what can be expected of that world which is actualized.

With this understanding of *possible* and *world*, I will argue this is the best of all possible worlds. I begin with the statement found in Genesis 1:3, where God surveyed all that He had created and pronounced it "very good." Granted, the text does not say explicitly that it was the best, only that it was very good. Grammatically, however, the word can mean moral goodness, in which case it is a statement affirming something of the intrinsic moral goodness of creation in comparative terms. The only standard to which it can be compared is God. In this sense, it cannot be best in any absolute sense because only God is best. (It has already been noted that creation cannot be substantively the same as the Creator). The fact, however, that the text provides the reader with this particular information is instructive in and of itself. God wanted humanity to know that regardless how things would appear at some time later, that when it came from the word of God, creation was very good. The evaluative statement is one made from the character of God whose judgment is perfect.

When God evaluates His creation, He does so as the omniscient, morally good One. His omniscience insures that He knows all things about creation. As the morally perfect One, He cannot lie or deceive. Further, the only point of reference from which to make the pronouncement is His own perfect character. When God pronounces something very good, "very" and "good" are the measurement of the One who is absolutely good. It is common understanding that the character of the one making an evaluative statement conveys something to the evaluative statement itself. For example, consider two people making a similar claim about different soups.

Suppose that on a very cold day a street person who has not eaten for a day is given some poorly made hot soup, and upon eating it, exclaims that it is very good. Also suppose a connoisseur of fine soups tastes soup made in his kitchen and upon tasting it pronounces it "very good." Surely one would not assume that the two soups are of equal quality. So it is with God. If God says that something is "very good," it is measured against His perfect character, which can only mean that it is the best. The statement is not about what creation would become or anything else; it is a statement about the substantive quality and moral ordering of what has been made. Moreover, if God does not do His best, then what is created lacks some logically possible perfection. Accepting Augustine and Aquinas on the point that evil is the lack in that which is good, it follows that if creation lacks some perfection possible to creation, then creation is in some sense evil from the beginning. This would mean that God is responsible for evil and that the concept of *very good* loses all normal meaning, for now something that lacks what it could have is called *very good* and our basic understanding of good and evil is neutralized.

There is a tacit assumption behind most denials that this is the best of all possible worlds that I find as rather incoherent. That is, the redeemed state is better than the initial state of creation. The argument here is that God is morally justified in allowing evil because through the redemption that is in Christ (a result of sin), redeemed man is elevated to a better state than possible through creation. To assume, however, that the state of the redeemed is a better state qualitatively than the state of man at the point of creation raises at least two concerns. First, the claim necessitates that God did not do His best at creation, in which case He is not the all-good God He claims to be. This means that either He chose not to do his best, in which case He is not all-good or that He wanted to create the best, but He could not. In that case, He is not omnipotent.

Second, if the Kingdom is a better state (I am not arguing there are no differences) than initial creation and if the Kingdom comes about because of sin with Christ's subsequent redemption, then sin is necessary to the best state. According to this line of thought, God is morally justified in requiring evil since from it He brings into being, by redemption, a better state for humanity (of course, not *all* humanity because as a result of sin, some people go to hell!). This requires that evil is necessary to the best world, which, if it does not make God the author of evil, it does make Him dependent on evil for doing what is best. Moreover, it seems questionable to affirm that the end of things, when measured against original creation, is either better or worse.

Possibly one could argue that it will be different, but intrinsically better is another matter altogether. When measured against what sin has done, this reasoning holds the end for the redeemed is better than the original state, making the Fall necessary. It seems theologically inappropriate to argue that the consequent (the Kingdom) justifies the antecedent in any case, but especially when the antecedent is evil. Even more alarming is the fact that all of this makes God dependent upon evil to do His best, which means God is not omnipotent.

If this world is not the best of all possible worlds, then one of the following must be true: (1) God chose not to do His best, which seems to question His goodness; (2) God did not know which world would be best, which questions His omniscience; (3) God knew which world would be the best and wanted to actualize it, but lacked the power to do so. This, of course, would question His power. All three possibilities seem unacceptable, leaving the only one possibility—this is the best of all possible worlds. Given the options, it seems to me that this must be the best of all possible worlds. After all, if God is able to bring about a greater good out of evil as G-G theodicies maintain, it would seem a small thing for God to bring the best world out of nothing.

According to Augustine and others, the best possible world is one in which man has libertarian freedom that has limits in the extent of its exercise. If it is possible to have a world from the beginning where man with libertarian freedom always did what was best and all loved God, that would be the world we would have. The best possible world should not be measured primarily on the standard of human felicity, but on the moral entailments of Kingdom of God itself—namely that for which man was created. Whatever achieves the best in this sense is what God actualizes. Theoretically, maybe we could say that the best world would be a world in which there is an optimal relationship between good and evil as defined by the Kingdom of God.

William Lane Craig suggests that, based upon middle knowledge, God "has actualized a world containing an optimal balance between saved and unsaved, and those who are unsaved suffer from transworld damnation."[31] If Craig is right on this point, it might shed some light on why this is the best of all possible worlds, an idea that seems to me to have both theological and philosophical legitimacy. If so, then it would also allow for the existence of gratuitous evil without counting against either God's knowledge or His moral character, as this would be the best of all possible worlds. If gratuitous evil existed in this world, we would know there is not another possible world where gratuitous evil did not exist. In addition, it seems to me that if this is not the best of all possible worlds, then even the G-G theodicies are in trouble. Consider; if this is not the best of all possible worlds, then there is a better world, a world where certain horrific evils would not exist. But if the possibility of such a world being feasible, and yet God does not actualize it, what does that say about God? It says He has a moral flaw, in which case, it seems that everything collapses.

SUMMARY

This chapter has outlined some worldview concepts necessary for the Creation-Order theodicy to have viability. The concepts discussed in this chapter lay the foundation for demonstrating how God in His sovereignty has established the rules for His interaction with man (the second actual mind) who has libertarian freedom. Libertarian freedom is necessary for man to love God, which is the highest function of man. If libertarian freedom exists, it seems reasonable to conclude that gratuitous evil could exist. Furthermore, these concepts explain how God manifests Himself in the realm of creation, which provides the framework by which the attributes of God are understood and expressed in contingent reality.

It also suggests how God's providence is worked out within the context of this creation order—the only place or time where there is need for divine providence, I might add. All of this provides for the latitude in the outworking of what we call *history,* where man can make real choices with real consequences, often resulting in gratuitous evil without counting against God morally or His creative purposes substantively. This will be the subject of the next chapter.

Admittedly, some of these ideas have their detractors; however, I believe there are convincing answers to the objections. However, if I am right, it seems this could be a way for understanding the existence of gratuitous evil, which as Ronald Nash says, would tip the balance in favor of the theist. I hope it is clear by now why the claim that this is the best of all possible worlds is important. If this is the best of all possible worlds, then the amount of gratuitous evil is at a minimal level, all other matters being considered. In addition, if this is the best of all possible worlds, God has created the very best that is possible to create. Remember, the main thrust of this chapter is to set the foundation for making the case that gratuitous evil is real, but does not count against the moral perfection of God. The next chapter shows how all of this fits together to craft the Creation-Order theodicy.

NOTES

1. This does not mean that the person necessarily lives as if God exists only that he thinks it is more likely that God exists than He does not exist.
2. There may be other forms of theism that are involved but all that is being defended here is trinitarian theism.
3. Certainly there are objective acts which are called evil acts, and in this sense people may think of evil as something of substance. This, however, is not what evil is fundamentally. It is only how a condition is manifested, and its manifestation causes human pain in an objective measurable way.
4. This does not mean that man always processes correctly, only that it is possible. Furthermore, the Fall has certainly impacted how man processes some information.
5. I am not attempting to determine the degree or extent of freedom in terms of antecedent causes. It seems that Christians could differ at this point and still be in agreement with the notion of libertarian freedom as defined here.
6. Thomas P. Flint, *Divine Providence: The Molinist Account* (Ithaca, NY: Cornell University, 1998), 34. He gives parameters to his understanding of libertarian traditionalism when he writes, "It seems more accurate to think of our free actions as invariably reactive—as responses to divine initiatives. Our movements may not be determined by the natural and supernatural influences to which we are subject, but the presence and power of such influences can hardly be gainsaid."
7. I am not suggesting that the unregenerate mind and regenerate mind have the same relationship with God or that they comprehend God in the same way, only that the mind of both function as authentic minds. However, the mind of both the regenerate and unregenerate have the same structure and are limited by the same creation ordering.
8. Udo Middelmann, *The Innocence of God* (Colorado Springs: Paternoster Press, 2007), 119.
9. Madeleine L'Engle, *A Wrinkle in Time* (New York: Dell, 1973 originally published Farra, Straus and Girous, Inc. in 1962), 198-9.
10. It will be assumed at this point that animals do not have the power of moral choice, although it is clear that they do make choices. The point would be that they do not make conscious moral choices based upon some objective moral criteria.
11. Gottfried Wilhelm Leibniz, *Theodicy*. Translated by E.M. Huggard from C.J. Gerhardt's Edition of the Collected Philosophical Works, 1878-1890 (LeSalle: Open Court, 1985), 135.
12. Consider the cursing of the fig tree where one sees some interruption in the normal flow of things. Of course a fig tree withering is not unusual, but as the disciples report, what caught their attention was that it happened so soon. Jesus was able to touch just a piece of reality and speed up the decaying process. If a law was broken, then all things under that law would have changed, as any law of nature is by definition universal. So, all things under the rule of decay should have withered. The only areas that seem off limits for God to touch are those things such as He has promised in Genesis nine. For example, He cannot destroy the world by flood and summer and winter will continue as will seed time and harvest.
13. Flint, *Divine Providence*, 38.
14. Ibid., 41.

15. Kenneth Keathley, *Salvation and Sovereignty* (Nashville: B & H Academic, 2010), 38.

16. For those interested in reading more about middle knowledge, I recommend the following: William Lane Craig, *The All Wise God* (Eugene, OR: Wipf and Stock Publishers, 2000); Jay Richards, The Untamed God (Downers Grove: InterVarsity Press, 2003); Thomas Flint, *Divine Providence: The Molinist Account* (Ithaca, NY: Cornell University, 1998); Terrance Tiessen, *Providence and Prayer* (Downers Grove: InterVarsity Press, 2000).

17. By feasible I mean that it is possible to think of a better world, but given all the factors involved in any world coming into existence there are some worlds that are not possible or they are not feasible. When I use the term possible worlds in this volume, I mean the same thing here as feasible worlds. I use possible worlds because this is the language used in much of the literature.

18. A. J. Vanderjagt, Gen ed., *Brill's Studies in Intellectual History*, vol. 7 *The Problem of Divine Foreknowledge and Future Contingents From Aristotle to Surarez*, by William Lane Craig (Leiden: E. J. Brill, 1988), 233.

19. Richard Swinburne, *Providence and the Problem of Evil* (Oxford, Clarendon Press), 8.

20. Bruce R. Reichenbach, *Evil and a Good God* (New York: Fordham University Press, 1982), 128.

21. Alvin Plantinga, "The Free Will Defense," in *Philosophy of Religion*, ed. Melville Y. Stewart (Sudbury, MA: Jones and Bartlett Publishers, 1996), 386.

22. Michael Peterson, *God and Evil* (Boulder,CO: Westview Press, 1998), 49.

23. David Blumenfeld, "Is The Best Possible World Possible?" *The Philosophical Review* 84 (April 1975): 165.

24. Ibid., 169. Blumenfeld argues on Leibniz's behalf saying: "It is, strictly speaking, possible that God should choose less than the best, though it is *certain* that he will not. Leibniz's motives for holding this view are clear: he wishes to preserve God's freedom and avoid the charge that this world is the only one that is (really) possible. How God's choice of the best can be contingent, given that he is by definition all-good, is a serious and well-known problem. But for our present purposes it is enough to note that Leibniz thought he had shown that it was certain that God would be determined by considerations of perfection: the more perfect a possible world, the greater it attractiveness to his will. So, it seems, if a given possible world were the most perfect, that would be a sufficient condition for God's choosing it."

25. Ibid., 163.

26. David Schrader, "Evil and the Best of Possible Worlds" *Sophia* 27 (July 1988): 27. It is not necessary to accept Schrader's total argument in order to use his notion of the best of possible worlds.

27. R.W.K. Patterson, "Evil, Omniscience and Omnipotence," *Religious Studies* 15 (March 1979): 2.

28. C. Mason Myers, "Free Will and the Problem of Evil," *Religious Studies* 23 (1987): 29.

29. Philip L. Quinn, "God, Moral Perfection and Possible Worlds" in Michael Peterson, ed. *The Problem of Evil* (Notre Dame: Notre Dame Press, 1992), 301.

30. Leibniz, *Theodicy*, 128.

31. Ibid.

6
CREATION-ORDER THEODICY

It is now possible to formulate what I have termed the Creation-Order (C-O) theodicy. This theodicy affirms all the attributes of God that G-G theodicies do. The difference is that G-G theodicies argue that gratuitous evil is only apparent, while the C-O theodicy claims gratuitous evil is real, but that it does not count against the moral perfection of God. The C-O theodicy argues that gratuitous evil is actual and God is morally justified in permitting such. Admitting to gratuitous evil in this way seriously weakens the argument from evil and lays a proper foundation for speaking to those who are suffering.

Rejecting the premise of G-G theodicies does not deny there are never any cases where God brings good from evil intent (or at least it appears that good has come from the evil). The objection here is that the evil is allowed for the purpose of bringing about a greater good.[1] Moreover, if the basic tenets of the C-O theodicy are right, then the atheist's argument is seriously undercut and the power of emotional skepticism often experienced by believers overridden. In the case of the C-O theodicy, the believer does not solace himself with the thought of some eventual good springing from his suffering, but rather he looks directly to the mercy and comfort of God Himself to sustain and encourage him in times of suffering (2 Cor 1:3–4; 12:9).

One difficulty of G-G theodicies when carried to their logical conclusion is that the very God who is to help in time of need is also the God who wills the suffering in the first place. In this case, God becomes at best like the Boy Scout who pushes the old lady into traffic so that he can save her, and at worst, something like a witch doctor (you can never be sure what you will get from him). Stated rather crassly, if it serves God's purposes to allow some terrible evil in your life, you should rejoice because His purposes are being served at your expense. I suggest that the C-O theodicy would avoid this tension.

THE CREATION-ORDER THEODICY

The argument from evil does not necessarily deny that there is some evidence for God's existence, but whatever that evidence is, the evidence from evil overpowers it or cancels it out. Primarily, the reason given by the atheist is that there is gratuitous evil in the world. According to the G-G theodicy, gratuitous evil cannot exist, as according to the theist, that would mean God is not sovereign over His creation. Remember, the G-G theodicy says that God only allows that evil in this world from which He can bring about a greater good or prevent a worse evil. As we said before, there is no way to confirm the latter part of that statement. So, what we have is God is morally justified in the evil He allows in this world because from it He will bring about a greater good. If there is no greater good (it is gratuitous), then God is not morally justified in allowing that evil. Of course, I am certainly in agreement that whatever happens on this earth is allowed by God. The question is, on what grounds is He justified in allowing it? Is it because He will bring a greater good from it—or is there another way to understand God's moral justification?

As I have argued, I believe there are too many attending problems to the G-G theodicy (chapter five), which means there must be other grounds on which God is justified in allowing evil in His creation. I believe there is and I have called it the Creation-Order Theodicy (C-O). I want to reiterate that we are not answering the question of why or how evil came into the world. The Bible is very clear on that—through one man's choice to disobey God sin entered the world (Ro 5:12). The question before us is why God continues to allow evil (sin) to run so rampant throughout His creation. The answer must not deny anything God affirms nor affirm anything God denies. I would say that how we answer this question has implications, even serious implications, for other doctrines Christians have traditionally believed. In fact, I think it is safe to say every theodicy touches all other major Christian doctrines, so this is no small matter.

The Created and Uncreated Reality Connection

When God sovereignly chose to create, He brought into existence a second circle of reality. Prior to creation, only one circle of reality existed—God (uncreated reality). Within this circle the perfect character of God meant a perfect relationship between the members of the Trinity. With the dawn of creation, however, a second circle of reality existed; this circle was different from, but compatible with, the first circle of reality. These are not unrelated circles, but rather now form different strata or aspects of reality. At creation and from that point on, there would be two circles of reality—the *contingent* reality circle of creation (created and material reality which is dependent upon another for its existence) and the *necessary* reality circle of God (uncreated and immaterial reality dependent upon no other for its existence). Contingent reality includes rational, personal man with a mind capable of authentic love, and moral judgment (among other things) because he has the power of moral choice or what we have called libertarian freedom.

In creation, the human mind is patterned after the divine mind and functions similar to God's mind (Gen 1:26), but necessarily (because of its created*ness)* at a diminished level since it is limited in knowledge and power (Is 55:8–9). God's necessary knowledge is intrinsic (His natural knowledge), and His knowledge of contingent reality is comprehensive (free knowledge), while man's knowledge is acquired and limited. Furthermore, man exists in a material context and God in an immaterial context. Although these two circles differ in certain respects, they are not contrary, for God created the material circle (including space and time) in such a way that it is compatible with what is immaterial. In this way God can occupy both without character distortion as the material does not squeeze out the immaterial. Moreover, He could be in, as well as act in, the space/time circle without conflict to His own being. We can clearly see this truth revealed in the Incarnation, where God lives and acts in time. Furthermore, once God takes on flesh (of the material world), He has this body forever and yet today Jesus is at the right hand of the Father—this shows the compatibility between the two circles.

As pointed out earlier, God's engaging creation legitimately requires some self-imposed restraint (not requiring any change in essence) in the way certain attributes of God are manifest in the material circle.[2] This intentional restraint does not diminish God*ness*, as can be seen in the Incarnation. Here, God becomes man without ceasing to be God and lives in the material circle without forfeiting His eternality (Phil 2:5–11). Moreover, Christ submitted to the will of men in the crucifixion because He submitted to the will of the Father that it should be so, but did so without damage to His own sovereignty (Matt 26:39, 42, 56). In this event, one witnesses divine sovereignty, love, justice, mercy, and human freedom all coming together without conflict. This was made possible by God's creation order. God so created and structured contingent reality with its corollary rules that not only does man have authentic freedom (libertarian freedom), but it is possible for God to live and act within His created order.

With the existence of creation, God's attributes express themselves under two conditions—within the circle of uncreated reality (unrestrained) and within the circle of created reality (restrained). While God is sovereign, His free choice (sovereignty) to give man libertarian freedom (I have also spoken of this as the power of moral choice and authentic freedom, and I mean to convey the same idea by all three within the material circle) does not limit Him in the uncreated circle, but only restrains the manifestation of sovereignty (and other attributes) in the created circle. The creation order design makes the interface possible between the circle of created reality and the circle of uncreated reality in such a way that both divine sovereignty and human freedom exist without impingement on the other or conflict between the two.

Once again, I point to the Incarnation, for there we see how the two circles operate. In the Incarnate Christ, divinity and humanity are bridged in one person with two natures (Constantinople 381). Man is made in the image of God and therefore there is compatibility between the nature of God and the nature of man even though they are different (not contradictory). One might say that they are the same in function (or mode), but difference in predication. In the Incarnation, God becomes a man without ceasing to be God. The nature of God and the nature of man co-exist, unmingled in one *person.* There is no tension, no conflict. The nature of God and the true (sinless) nature of man existed without creating a dual person. The Incarnation is possible because man is created in the image of God, which is part of creation order.

As there is order within the circle of uncreated reality there is a similar order in created reality which is predicated on the order of uncreated reality. This is necessary if the two circles are to interact in an authentic way. Whereas in uncreated reality, the order within the Trinity is so because of the perfect nature of God, in created reality, order must be *prescribed* as a creative act. Without established order, chaos would result both in the moral and physical realm, which would then render God's intention to interact meaningfully with man impossible (Amos 3:3; 2 Cor 6:14). God, in His divine wisdom and grace, created just such an ordering that maximizes creation's potential while remaining compatible with His divine attributes. In this way, God is able to act in the material circle without abuse of or conflict with His God*ness*. Man is made capable of enjoying his creaturely freedom, making it possible for him to know God relationally and to love Him. This is part of the creation order.

As an aside I will add that this is to the great glory and grace of our God. When man functions well in his authentic freedom, he glorifies God, for this is the intention and plan of God. The glory of God is not that He determined everything, but that He has created in such a way that it gives man the wonderful potential of obeying and loving God as a matter of choice as well as contributing something to the flow of human history.

Some might protest such a position entails that not everything that happens on this earth has a divine purpose. If this is so, the argument continues God is not sovereign and there are happenings in human history that have no purpose, meaning we live in a chaotic world. I have already addressed the sovereignty complaint, and the charge of historical chaos is answered on the same grounds. That is, *purpose* is not the only thing explaining events in history. Some events such as the Holocaust may not have a purpose, but they do have a reason. That is, we can explain why the Holocaust happened. Because it can be explained, it is not chaotic.

As pointed out earlier, there is a difference between *reason* and *purpose,* and it is a distinction that must be maintained in the discussion of evil. God's creation order assures nothing is chaotic (unexplainable); there is always a reason, if not a purpose. Therefore, it seems to me the complaint that everything on earth must have a purpose is silenced. In addition, given the infinite wisdom, goodness, and power of God (Eph 1:5; Rom 11:33), it seems reasonable to conclude that this is the best of possible creation orders. This includes both the moral and physical ordering of creation, which is to say that creation order optimizes the function of creation and its interaction with the Creator as well as its conformity with the counsels of God. If this is correct, then once God establishes the creation order, it is within this order that He works when interacting within the material circle. To do otherwise would abandon what is optimum, as well as His own rules.

Although God clearly has the power and prerogative (theoretically) to act in any way consistent with His character, He submits that power and prerogative to the creation order established by His wisdom and power. Looking at God acting in the circle of uncreated reality (the society of divine persons), the only limits are His own character. However, to speak of God acting within the circle of created reality, one must recognize the parameters of His intentionally established creation order. Therefore, when addressing the expressed possibilities of God's sovereignty and power and what they would look like, one must be careful to consider which circle of reality is in view. God must abide by that to which He voluntarily commits Himself when first choosing to create. To violate His own creation order would mean going against Himself, something the faithful Creator will not do.

Those who counter that creation order disallows miracles and makes God appear as a deistic God must remember the discussion in chapter five. There I noted that the creation order allows for God's intervention under certain circumstances in a way consistent with creation order. This would include the possibility of miracles. In the scheme of the creation order, God's providential involvement in creation is a very important part of that order. God's providential involvement is not to rescue creation from some unknown state of affairs, as God knows all things. Instead, it is what assures that man's libertarian freedom never foils God's ultimate end for man. It also makes possible prayer; for instance, man can pray to God and God can intervene in history in response to that prayer. Of course, that regards only those prayers asking God to do what He can do within the rules of creation order and His own character.

This creation is not an experiment by God to see how things will turn out. Experiments by their very nature indicate a lack of knowledge on the part of the one doing the experiment. The one who is experimenting does so because he is not sure how things work or turn out. That is not true of God as He knows all things. He therefore does not need to experiment. God is the faithful omniscient Creator who established the creation order by His wisdom, goodness and power. Therefore, God will never abandon His own ordering, nor will He alter things because He found a better way to do things.

Sovereign God, Vassal Man

God's choice to create entails, at least in part, that creation is compatible with His being. This means creating man as a rationally functioning personal being capable of authentic love and moral judgment. As a rationally functioning moral personal being, man enjoys creaturely freedom in order that he might authentically (freely) choose to love God (among other things). The creation of man in God's image, however, requires a certain creation-order design whereby the two minds can intersect and interact as two legitimately constituted and functioning minds.

I think too little has been made of this fact—man is made in the image of God (Gen 1:26; 9:6; Ja 3:9). I know evangelicals are quick to point to this fact when speaking of abortion (or the special nature of human life) as a way to firm up the argument that man has worth and significance. Of course, I agree with that totally. What is lacking, however, is the application of that truth on a more fundamental level. The idea is that because man is made in the image of God, we are to treat man with respect, dignity, and celebrate his uniqueness. Man is special, and when we denigrate man, we denigrate God. To make man of no value by reducing him to a zero (something Francis A. Schaeffer always rejected, as he would say, "man is not a zero") in order to magnify God's glory is incoherent and theologically infantile.

There is confusion here with respect to the effects of sin and the reality of a special creation of God. While on the one hand I affirm that man is a sinner, born alienated from God, who can do no good thing for his salvation, on the other hand, I argue his uniqueness should be celebrated as a wonderful creation of God. I would suggest that this truth has been belittled by both Darwinian evolution and the present-day theological excesses of the doctrine of total depravity. What happened to man in the Garden changed his relationship with God, but it did not substantively change his humanness, which is what I suggest is to be celebrated.

Furthermore, I believe that the power of choice given to mankind is one aspect of humanness that makes man so unique that to deny the wonder and greatness of this aspect is to denigrate God's creation. It is true that man has used this power of choice to go against God; however, this is only the misuse of that wonderful gift. We do not celebrate what man does, but we should celebrate who he is essentially. What he is, essentially, is made obvious by God placing him over creation as a vassal, allowing him to care for creation, and to love and worship God.

Whereas God would place man over the other creatures on earth (Gen 1:26–31), man would function as God's vassal. The finite mind (man) governs over the circle of created reality on behalf of the infinite mind (God). The purpose of the creation order is to establish boundaries and guiding principles for both God and man, through which the vassal can actually govern earth, but in such a way as not to confound the rule of the Sovereign.

The genius of the creation order is that it gives man libertarian freedom in a way that is authentic. This authentic power to choose makes it possible for man to love and obey God. It also, unfortunately so, leaves the opportunity for man to disobey God. Of course, because it is a real choice, real consequences follow. This possibility of disobeying God means that such disobedience will have real consequences. We know that in the first case, disobedience brought death into the human race even as God said it would. Here we see the first sign of creation order working. In time, we see man using his freedom to commit acts of gratuitous evil (Gen 4:8–12), where sad consequences result. The consequences of this disobedience often results in gratuitous evil.

The creation order does not provide a means for God to filter out the bad choices from which He cannot bring about a greater good. Instead, the creation order allows for gratuitous evil as a corollary to the authenticity of the libertarian freedom. Gratuitous evil does not alter the counsels of God as God is at work, providentially working all things according to His counsels. This does not mean that He uses everything, but that nothing can set in motion a chain of events that ultimately affects the end as God has planned it. Creation order is crafted so that real human choices bring real consequences without negating the counsels of God. Furthermore, the created order makes possible God's providential work and His personal care for His created beings. He can do this without sacrificing man's libertarian freedom. Therefore, at no time does gratuitous evil jeopardize the counsels of God or exceed the providential power of God.

God's Control and Man's Freedom

God, who is neither chaotic in nature nor in deed, necessarily creates and rules in an orderly fashion. He does this through his creation order. This order is necessary to the harmonious physical and moral function of creation[3] and His personal interaction with creation.[4] It appears that in order for there to be a *stable* created environment in which God and man interact in a purposeful way, only two possibilities exist. One method would be where God determines *everything*, thus assuring the order of creation based on divine predetermination, which would result in social stability. A second way for God to provide for the suitable function of creation is by establishing certain moral (internal) and physical (external) ordering consonant with man's libertarian freedom. Determining all things necessarily eliminates man being made in God's image (God is not a determined being). This would be an ordering that He would maintain in His omnipotence.

You will remember I mentioned this earlier when I spoke about the different means of control. *Control* is used here in the sense that a man has control over his automobile by the means of the steering mechanism, and control in the sense that a man has control over his family: there are rules that form the outer boundary of behavior, but within those bounds there is individual freedom. I have suggested the latter is the more appropriate way to view God's control over His creation. The former is both anti-intuitive as well as difficult to square with the Bible, where there are many references to man given the choice over something—even serving God (Deut 30:15–19; Josh 24:15; Prov 1:29; 1 Kings 18:21; Is 56:4).

We all sense we have choices in life, choices that make a difference. If we do not have choices but only think we do, then God has created a world of deception, and one can be sure of nothing. In fact, the Church Father's, for the first 300 years at least, believed man had libertarian freedom. As Augustine said, "A runaway horse is better than a stone." Still, man's libertarian freedom is not absolute. It has boundaries established by creation order, which is one way God controls the direction of history. A second way is by limiting the types and number of choices given to man.

The Principle of Cause and Effect

Among other things, creation order assures that given certain human actions, particular consequences follow. This is often referred to as the law of the harvest (Gal 6:7), or in the physical realm, as cause and effect. In some cases, it is possible for God to reverse the intent of a certain event, but not the act itself. Joseph's experience is an example of this. In this story, the evil intent of the brothers is reversed and God brings about something totally different (an example of God's providential involvement). God did not determine that the brothers sell Joseph into slavery, but in His providence He intervenes without changing the brothers' choices. It was a bad thing and the brothers bear the responsibility. Although in the end something good comes of this, still, Joseph really suffers as a result of their evil actions. Their bad choices caused a very bad effect. The fact that in the end, God uses Joseph in Egypt to do a good thing, whatever good that comes is not *because of* the evil of the brothers, but *in spite of* the evil. It is only the intent, not the suffering that is reversed through God's intervention, as stated by Joseph himself.

In other cases, however, the evil intent is matched by evil consequences; for reasons known only to God, He did not intervene. Creation order does not require intervention in every case, but it does make allowances for such. Furthermore, God has not committed Himself to intervene in every case of evil, and therefore, such cases as Joseph should not be used as a normative paradigm. What it does show is that God is able to do such. One can think of many examples from history where God did not intervene, such as the Holocaust. In fact, when we look at human history, it seems that the norm is that God does not intervene to reverse consequences. That should not be understood as my saying God is not involved. I am only saying He is not involved in reversing and bringing some good from it all.

One can consider the situation found in Luke 13:1–5. Here the murderous intent of Herod results in terrible consequences for the worshipers. The point Jesus makes from this incident is instructive. Jesus does not indicate that the intent is reversed or that some good results from the evil. The worshipers died, and no comfort is given that some greater good obtained because of it. Instead, Jesus uses the event to teach us that we should be prepared to die at any point, since the evil intentions of others can spell death for their victims without notice. It teaches that we live in a fragile world and must be prepared to face eternity. It seems clearly that this account given by Luke is an example of gratuitous evil.

It is interesting to note that God gives commands that govern how one treats others. When the neighbor is treated with love and respect, gratuitous evil is minimized. The moral commands are codified aspects of the creation order by which man is instructed to live rightly in his material existence. When we live rightly, gratuitous evil is minimized because the effect of godly acts is that people are helped, not harmed. This is another aspect of creation order.

Could God Prevent All Horrific Evils?

The question that may come at this point is whether it is possible that God could prevent the most horrific evils and still honor libertarian freedom. If one asks this question from the perspective of God's power, the answer is *yes*; that is to say, no individual or group act is beyond the reach of God. However, as we have seen, God's work within creation is not just about His power; it is about how He will manifest His power within the circle of created reality in light of creation order. When answering this question we must not just look at God for who He is, but at how He works within the circle of created reality. Remember, we get a hint of this when we look at the Incarnation.

Let's think through the question in terms of what the question entails. First, horrific evils are horrific because this is how they look in comparison to other evils. When one says that this or that evil is "horrific", he is saying that it is a worse evil than some other kind of evil. It could be worse in number or in kind; it really makes little difference to our discussion. A conclusion drawn from comparison of evils is determined by the perspective of the one drawing the conclusion. For example, Hitler thought that the existence of an inferior race was a greater evil than exterminating the race. While many disagree, the point is that what might be a horrific evil for one person might not be for another person. When asking God to prevent the worse of evils, it is necessary to determine whose standard of morality will be used to conclude which evils should be prevented. At this point it might be rather difficult to achieve any consensus, and we will see that it is really on a very personal level that we ask this question. So, from the beginning we have the problem of consensus regarding which evils should be classified as *horrific*.

Another problem arises when one thinks through the logic of the question. If a horrific evil is horrific because of how it compares to another evil, then logically this will mean that all evil should be prevented. Consider the following argument.

Suppose we represent the evil in the world by X and the varying degrees of evil by X+1, X+2, X+3 and so forth, where the higher the number associated with X, the worse the evil. X+3 is a worse evil than X+1. For argument's sake, let's also assume that X+5 is the worse evil imaginable to man. Man requests that God prevent X+5. The request is for God to prevent the evil before it happens (this in itself poses a problem, but is another discussion for another time. This means it will never have been a part of the human experience—right? The request is to stop it, which would mean it never happened or was just on the verge of happening. Assuming God prevents X+5, the worst evil in the human experience will be X+4. However, when the same logical procedure is applied to X+4 as was to X+5, the worst evil in the human experience is now X+3. Taken to its logical conclusion, the request would not stop until God has prevented all evil. That is, we would have a world with no evil, but if that were possible, that is the world we would have.

We know that people really do choose to do evil, which means there are evil consequences played out in human history. If I am right in the argument above, however, it would mean that all evil choices would never obtain or the evil choice would not bring about the normal consequence. This would invalidate the principle of cause and effect, which is stated in Galatians 6:7. If this would be the case, then one of the key elements of authentic choice, which is its corollary consequences, would be canceled out. This would seem to bring about a serious impingement on the authenticity of libertarian freedom, if not destroying it altogether. The other possibility would be that the only choices people would be permitted to make would be the choices resulting in good. The same critique as above would follow, and in the end, libertarian freedom would be destroyed and we would be locked into a mechanistic world, both morally and physically. A further inescapable result would be that God is responsible for evil.

I am not suggesting God never intervenes, as I think it is quite likely that He often does providentially interfere preventing some evil, but the standard there would be different. It would not be to guarantee there would be no gratuitous evil in the world. He might be moved to act providentially because a particular evil would move history outside the bounds of creation order (an example of this would be Tower of Babel, but here choices were not abrogated; they were limited). Or it might be that God intervenes on behalf of the prayers of His people. There may be other reasons for His intervention, but not on the basis of stopping the most horrific evils or not by removing man's libertarian freedom. Furthermore, the choice would still be made; it is only that God would reverse the evildoers' wicked intentions, such as what happens on the Cross. So, I conclude that for several reasons, under the present creation order it is meaningless to say God could prevent all the horrific evils on earth without impinging on man's libertarian freedom.

Social Justice

Libertarian freedom seems necessarily attached to idea of social justice, and the idea of social justice subverts the basic tenet of the G-G theodicy (if all evil is allowed by God for from it He will bring about a greater good, then the evil should not be stopped, for in doing so, the good would be stopped). The Bible, however, is clear on the fact that God desires each man to act righteously (Micah 6:8) as well as to defend others against evil (1 Thess 5:15). Precisely in this way God intends to minimize gratuitous evil. Given the corruption of man's heart and man's power of moral choice, gratuitous evil does exist. Furthermore, wherever and whenever man in general and the believer in particular fails to stand against evil (as in the case of the Holocaust or slavery in the United States), gratuitous evil can grow very large and ugly. It reminds us that things are not the way they ought to be. In fact, such horrific gratuitous evil is a clear reminder of the wickedness of the human heart which should cause the Christian to renew his resolve to stand against social and moral evil. We can see how this strengthened the resolve of our country to do everything to prevent what happened on 9/11 from happening again.

The two planes striking the Trade Towers on September 11, 2001, was an example of gratuitous evil flowing from evil choices, leading to evil acts. It happened because a few people made certain decisions and it was within their power to carry out those wicked plans. Or the little girl who was abducted, raped and buried alive is another case in point. A man acted on wicked thoughts. It was his choice to abuse this little girl—he was not determined to do it. In fact, that is the very reason he was brought to trial and held legally accountable for his actions. Society operates on the notion that men are responsible for their actions. In fact, the early Church Fathers believed in libertarian freedom precisely for the fact they were ultimately responsible to God.

One can see the outworking of gratuitous evil in the case of those killed by the falling of the tower in Siloam and Pilate's hideous slaughter of those offering a sacrifice in worship (Lk 13:1–5). The first appears to be a natural evil. It might have been the result of poor workmanship, but we are not told. So, I will assume it is simply a natural evil. The latter event was the wicked choice of Pilate. In both cases people are killed. According to Jesus, the lesson here is not that some good comes from the evil (whether natural or moral), but rather that life is fragile and one never knows when death might unexpectedly take him. Therefore, all men should be prepared for life after death.

These examples instruct the living in a very forceful way that today is the day of salvation—"except you repent you shall likewise perish." There are no guarantees in this life. In at least one of these examples, a person made an evil choice that led to the untimely death of others—and a cruel death I might add. The intent is evil and the consequences are evil. The choices of those involved are freely made and intentionally evil.[5] Such choices and subsequent results stand as an example of potential evil within man, and the power that man has to cause great harm or great good in this age. Jesus is an example of one who used His human will to bring about a great good, while Herod illustrates the use of the power to bring about the great evil of the slaughtering of newborns (Matt 2:16). It is the potential of the power of libertarian freedom that makes possible both authentic good and real evil, including gratuitous evil.

God intends for man to exercise his power of choice to do what is right and stand against evil. The C-O theodicy argues that the very fact Christians are commanded to stand against evil is a strong indication that gratuitous evil exists. If all evil allowed by God necessarily becomes an evil that brings about a greater good, then the only evil present in the world would be God-allowed evil. Should the believer be successful in preventing this evil, he would also defeat the good that would have come from that evil. Whereas the good that is prevented is a necessary good, God must find another way for the good to obtain. Either the world would forever be minus that good or God would need to find another evil to bring it to pass. Whatever alternative way God chooses could not be by means of a greater evil. If it is a lesser evil, then the question is why did God not use the lesser evil in the first place? If it is an evil of equal weight, why is it not defeated, as in the first case?

The Bible indicates that Christians should stand against all evil and defeat it where possible. If God wants evil stopped (either by some external deterrent or by personal choice), then it must not be necessary for some good to obtain. At times (probably more often than not) evil is not stopped—not because it was designed as the means to some good, but because men are evil and often disobedient to God's Word. It is this evil that falls into the category of *gratuitous*. Out of this category of evil, God at times will accomplish some good. Most often, this happens in spite of the evil, not because of it. Furthermore, the good obtained under these circumstances is not a necessary good and could have been accomplished without the evil or by different circumstances. If the concept of creation-order is right, gratuitous evil does not count against God morally. In fact, it is just the opposite. It reflects His faithfulness to the order He has created rather than a system of predetermined motion.

Libertarian Freedom as Necessary for Authentic Love

John Hick's point that human freedom is necessary for man to love God seems convincingly argued. The C-O theodicy maintains that, without controversy, man loving God is man's highest calling. Next to it comes man loving his neighbor (Matt 22:37–40). It is impossible for any human response that is coerced or compelled in any manner to be defined as love. By definition, love is a free response. If it is not free, it is not love. However, the potential to love entails the possibility of the opposite. One who has the power of moral choice must be free to choose *not* to love God or his neighbor, as well as to love either or both. This fact is made clear in Genesis 4, where Abel freely chose to love and obey God, while Cain freely chose to disobey God (not loving God). As a consequence of the choice to disobey God, Cain also hated his brother and chose to do him bodily harm. Cain's choice was free (Gen. 4:7). Consequently, he was held accountable for it, as seen in Genesis 4:11–14. It is possible to obey God without loving God, but if we love God, we will obey Him. Jesus said that if we love Him, we will keep His Word (Jn 14:23–24).

Hick's point is a most important one for understanding humanity and its relationship to God. It is possible for God to create man to always do what God wants Him to do. That is, man could have been created so that he could only do what is right. In this case, doing right would not be by choice, but rather by a determinative creative act of God. However, it is impossible for God to determine that man will love Him. The only way to make love an authentic possibility for man would be to give man the power of choice. Authentic love is the highest function of mankind. It is bound up in the two great commandments (Matt 22:37–40). Paul says that love is the fulfillment of the whole law because love does no evil to his neighbor (Rom 13:10). To love requires the power to choose either to love or not to love, which arguably is a moral choice.

The Righteous Suffer for Righteousness Sake

When considering evil that results from evil human choices, it is important to understand the context in which the Bible speaks of such evils and subsequent suffering. The C-O theodicy does not deny that in some cases good does come out of evil; that is, not all evil is gratuitous. It maintains that should a good obtain, that does not provide evidence that the good is the moral justification for God permitting the evil. If a good obtains, it may be the providential work of God reversing some evil intent. Surely, Peterson's notion of character-building or Swinburne's idea of the good-of-being-used (or any of the other many suggestions of what the good might be) may have merit in some instances of evil. There is no objection to the claim that in some cases this can be observed. The C-O theodicy only contends that the good obtained is not a necessary good and that the evil is not necessary to the good. It can be thought of as a providential good. Moreover, the C-O theodicy argues that there is no way to demonstrate that the good would not have obtained without the evil. Furthermore, only when the believer suffers for righteousness sake can there be any assurance that God is working it out for good.

The C-O theodicy maintains there are two distinct categories, broadly speaking, under which a Christian may experience suffering. One category of suffering is that which comes to the believer because of righteous living. The other category is when a Christian suffers because of the brokenness of this age. When suffering under the former category, the believer can be assured that God is at work to reverse evil intent against him and bring good to him either in this life or the age to come. This is the only condition, however, that God promises to work in this way on behalf of the sufferer. This appears to be the teaching of Scripture as seen in several texts on suffering. Matthew 5:11 records the Lord's teaching that those who suffer "for My sake" are blessed. In James 1:3, James tells believers that in "the testing of your faith" you can rejoice. Peter reminds believers that when they suffer, they can rejoice, as it demonstrates the "genuineness of your faith" (1 Pet 1:7). In 2 Timothy 3:12, Paul says those who "desire to live godly" will suffer persecution, but the text says nothing about it being necessary in order for some good to obtain.

Suffering is a fact when men live righteously, especially in an unrighteous community (Is 59:14–15). Consider the following examples: Job suffered because of his righteousness (Job 1:10), Joseph because of his faithful proclamation of God's dreams to him (Gen 37:19—"Look, this dreamer is coming"), Shadrach, Meshach, and Abed-Nego for not worshiping the golden image (Dan 3:8–25), and Daniel for praying to God (Dan 6:10–23). The causal agent for the suffering in each case may be different. But in each case, the target was a righteous person and the reason was his righteous living. In each case the peaceable fruit of righteousness prevails.

It does seem that there is sufficient biblical warrant to claim that some believers' suffering is a direct result of the powers of darkness. Consider 2 Corinthians 12:7; Ephesians 6:12; 1 Peter 5:8 as testimony to the fact that our adversary seeks to destroy us. A word of caution is in order at this point. I hear Christians always blaming the devil for all the difficulty in their lives, which I believe is an overstatement. If we are honest, much of our suffering is because of our own silly choices. It is doubtful that it is the Devil who gives you cancer because you are a Christian. So, while one must recognize that it is possible that Satan is a source of our suffering at points, it is very difficult to say *when*.

When Christians suffer for righteousness sake (whether from Satan or other sources), God is at work to work things together for ultimate good as reckoned in the terms of the economy of His Kingdom. Then, it is *in spite* of the evil, not *because of* the evil. Christians will suffer in this world (as our Lord did), and the Spirit of God speaks to the matter of suffering for righteousness sake and encourages the Christian by informing him there is a blessedness for those who suffer accordingly. Romans 8:12–39 is a case in point.

Here Paul speaks about suffering for righteousness sake. In the middle of the discussion, he encourages believers "that all things work together for good to those who love God, to those who are called according to His purpose" (Rom 8:28). Later, he reminds Christians there is nothing that can separate them from the love of God which is in Christ Jesus our Lord (Rom 8:35–39). Cataloging different possibilities of suffering such as famine or nakedness, the context of the text all points to the fact that suffering results from living righteously. Paul concludes by encouraging the Christian that nothing can separate them from the love of God in Christ. In other words, do not stop living rightly just because you are mistreated because what is important is none of it can separate you from the love of God.

Hebrews 11:36–40 gives a similar account. The point is that the Christian should not compromise his faithfulness to the Lord just because it might result in some form of suffering. Instead, the Christian should live boldly for Christ, noting that nothing can separate him from the love of God. According to 2 Corinthians 1:3–7, Christians can also be assured that the Father of mercies and God of all comfort is present to encourage and comfort them when the "sufferings of Christ abound" in them (v. 5). While these verses speak of blessedness, things working out for good, and/or rejoicing in the midst of suffering, they are always in the context of suffering for righteousness. It seems inappropriate to apply these truths to situations where Christians suffer because of the brokenness of this world. This includes such things as cancer, heart attacks, and a variety of other diseases. This is not to say there is no word from God concerning such suffering, only that the verses mentioned do not address suffering in this category.

The Righteous Suffer From the Brokenness of This Age

Many of God's people have suffered because they live in this fallen place where things are terribly out of joint. The broken phase of this world is rather overwhelming at times. Evil can be very ugly and damaging, both on personal and national levels. The presence of such suffering is due to sinful choices, the wicked works of the god of this age, and the fallen*ness* in general (all of creation is out of joint—Romans 8:21–22). One gets a feel for the general fallen*ness* when reading Genesis 3:16–19. It is precisely this fallen*ness* that accounts for some (even *much*) suffering for both the believer and the unbeliever.

God forewarned the first parents in the Garden that "in the day you eat of it you shall surely die" (Gen 2:17). There are, however, many wonderful verses concerning God's help in time of need that serve to encourage the believer in difficult times (such as Ps 23:4; Ps 73:23–26; 2 Cor 12:9; or 1 Pet 5:7). It is precisely the love and care of the Lord Himself on which the believer should rest, and not the idea that some good will come from cancer or whatever form of suffering that might be involved. For the believer, there is help through trusting in God's grace and comfort in the midst of the suffering. While trusting in God, the believer does what he can to mitigate the effects of the suffering (Gen 39:14–40:14) and looks forward to the day of redemption when all will be made new (Rev 21:3–5).

According to the C-O theodicy, even when Christians suffer because of the brokenness of this present age, there is still opportunity for good in the Kingdom. This is not to say that the suffering comes in order for the good. Rather, in the flow of life when the suffering comes, the Christian can respond in such a way that his testimony in suffering points people to God. Christians, who live by God's grace in the midst of their suffering, are a testimony to God's mercy and comfort. By this, unbelievers may come to believe in God, and a wayward Christian might return to the Lord. The person who suffers might also give a testimony thanking God for the suffering if he believed it plays some positive part in his spiritual life. In such cases, the testimony is legitimate, but it is not the basis for a theodicy. Furthermore, the only person who has a right to testify in such a way is the person who suffered. This is not something that can be used to comfort others who are suffering, for in other cases there is no assurance that this good or any good may obtain. However, other Christians can be encouraged by the testimony of the reality of God's mercy and comfort in the midst of suffering.

The point of the C-O theodicy is that a testimony is not the basis for a theodicy. Suffering does not always result in a believer's spiritual welfare, as much depends on how he responds to the suffering. Over the years serving as a pastor, I have seen Christians go through tough times, and they were spiritually stronger as a result. On the other hand, I have seen an equal number who gave up on God in such times. Furthermore, just because some good comes from suffering, one cannot argue that either the suffering was necessary to the good or that the good would not have obtained without the suffering. In addition, if the evil is allowed by God in order to bring about the good, then it appears counter to pray for the healing of that person. Because it maintains that gratuitous evil exists, the C-O theodicy would teach consistently that there is purpose in praying for such a person that he might be healed. I hope you can begin to see that the C-O theodicy is consistent with the way we intuitively respond to suffering—with prayer, moral outrage, and efforts to put an end to it.

Of course, there are many cases of suffering that involve the unbeliever. In cases of intense, devastating suffering, the unbeliever is left to his own strength to survive. I am often amazed at how resilient the human soul is. I think this speaks to the wonder of humanity, and quite possibly, the common grace of God. Often, I hear Christians say they do not understand how anyone without the Lord can face such suffering. The fact is, many do, and they move on with life.

In some cases, when faced with extreme difficulty, the unbeliever is instructed in the fragility of life and his own mortality, leading him to repentance and turning to faith in Christ. However, even should this happen, it should not be used as a theological explanation for why the evil was allowed. The fact is it would only be a guess as there would be no way of knowing. It is even possible under this scenario that the person himself would testify he is thankful for the suffering because it brought him to Christ. While this is a legitimate testimony for the individual, it is not a theodicy. One can think of many who have publicly so testified and such a testimony should not be disallowed. To say, however, that God allowed that evil for this purpose is going beyond revelation and should not be a basis for a theological position. There have been many who have suffered and as a result, have become deeply embittered against God (Pharaoh is a case in point).

Natural Evil

It appears that much of natural evil falls into the category of suffering because of the fallen*ness* of this present age. An example of natural evil is found in Luke 13:4, which reports that 18 persons were killed when the tower in Siloam fell on them. One can imagine different explanations for the tower falling (probably due to deterioration), but the text does not give such information. Since Jesus makes no reference, it is assumed that it was not a moral lapse on the part of the engineers who designed the tower. The falling appears to have happened without warning or mischievous activity on the part of any particular person. The text states merely that it happened. Some people asked Jesus why such things should happen.

He does not suggest that the evil is allowed in order that some good might obtain. Instead, he points out that things like this happen. The story provides instruction for all persons to be prepared to die at any time. The text does not even say that God allows it for this purpose, only that such things happen, and this is one lesson to be learned from it. It is not necessary, however, to learn this lesson from only such events. The course of life is sufficient to establish the fact that death can come unpredictably at any moment. Furthermore, the Bible teaches the same lesson. While one may see such truth reinforced by the events of life, the events of life are not necessary to know the truth.

Of course, all natural evils do not fall neatly into this category. God might allow some natural events to bring judgment on a person or persons. In such incidences as famine and earthquake[6] in the Old Testament, God offers a word to explain why such things are happening, so it is not left up to the imagination of men to determine the purpose of the event. One must be very careful today in crediting such natural evils as God's judgment. (This is not to say they are not, only that there would be no way to know unless there was a word from God).

Some made this mistake following the September 11th massacre at the Trade Towers. They immediately proclaimed that it was a judgment of God on America for her sins (particular sins were even mentioned). However, it seems the evidence from the event warrants no such conclusion. Later, there were those who felt constrained to change their pronouncements because they realized there was simply no way to determine if this was the case. (Of course, pressure from supporters may have also contributed to the retraction).

Moreover, some evils are the result of moral lapses in humans. Consider the case where a contractor uses inferior materials to build a public building and later it collapses, killing many people. On its face, this is a natural disaster. There is no guarantee that a building will collapse if inferior materials are used, although it could be the cause. Consider another case where a famine occurs because politicians embezzle money earmarked for land conservation, leaving the land without proper management. It would be difficult to argue that hundreds of deaths in a collapsed building were worth it so that stricter inspections would be imposed. Sure, such an incident might save lives in the future, but hardly is the death of innocents necessary to make a building safer. In fact, such events have happened and stricter regulations were not enforced. One would also be hard-pressed to make the case that God allows thousands to die or suffer from malnutrition (usually children) if it leads to the politicians being brought to justice (or any other good one might think up). Such a good would hardly justify such a horrific evil. Furthermore, once the lesson is learned, the purpose for the evil would be served and the evil would disappear. Clearly, this is not the case.

Finally, from a Christian perspective, Satan can cause natural evils (Job 2:18–19) and may have influence in the evil choices of men (Rev 16:13–16). I have not spent much time on the role of Satan and the powers of darkness as a cause suffering; it is not because I think it is not a possibility. The reason for little attention is because it is very difficult to know when something like that happens. So I will admit that some evil in this world is the work of the god of this age, but even still, there is little or no biblical reason for claiming that it was allowed for some greater good. In the first place, it is very difficult to lay causation at the feet of Satan with any sense of certainty. Second, as with all other evil, there is no warrant to say that it was allowed by God for some greater good.

The C-O theodicy explains such evils simply as the outworking of evil choices with horrific consequences within God's created order. They are not allowed by God in any active sense but in a passive sense, as this is the way things work within the structure of the creation order. Death and disease are enemies of God, as can be seen in the Lord's response when on earth: He weeps at the tomb of Lazarus (Jn 11:35) and raises the widow of Nain's son without any appeal from the crowd (Lk 7:14). The heart of God is grieved when the innocent are harmed. He does not countenance it in any way by bringing some good from it and then say, "See, that suffering was worth the good." It is not that God is powerless according to His power to do something, but that He has established the creation order within which He must interact with His creation. In some cases, according to the good pleasure of God, divine protection may be given, but it is not promised, nor should it necessarily be expected. If it comes, then praise belongs to God as it is for His purposes. What can be expected is that in all situations He never leaves nor forsakes His own (Heb 13:5–6).

Suppose that God intervened and prevented every horrific evil, which would *not* bring about some greater good. Under such circumstances, choices would not be choices because the appropriated consequences would not follow. This, however, is precisely what the G-G theodices require. If the only evil allowed by God is that which brings about a good, then He must prevent all other evils. At what point should He not intervene, and for whom should He intervene and on what basis? The fact is there is no way to answer this question because the G-G theodices are built on a faulty assumption. The sad fact is that in this present age there is much suffering and a large measure of it is gratuitous, which seems to be exactly what one would expect in a place alienated from God. The Christian can have hope in the Day to come when righteousness will rule in this world and can know the mercy and comfort of God until that time.

The Best of All Possible Worlds

I will suggest that given the understating of the world put forth here, gratuitous evil was present in all worlds possible. Before there was anything but God, all possible worlds existed as ideas in the mind of God. God's natural knowledge (eternal knowledge) informed Him on what worlds were possible and what worlds were not possible. All worlds possible were structured according to the same creation-order design as were certain events, such as the Cross (Rev 13:8). (Remember, in chapter five we saw that a world where all moral creatures always do right is not a possible world). In all worlds, man is limited in what choices he will have as well as what would be possible for him ontologically. In all possible worlds man has the power of moral choice. God, informed by middle knowledge, saw all counterfactuals of creaturely freedom and, consequently, all possible worlds as they unfold based upon the choices of men within the prescribed limits. Each world includes (but is not limited to) men's choices, men's prayers, God's responses to prayers, His interventions, His persuasive acts among men, and certain predetermined events which are part of all possible worlds—everything that pertains to the creation-order design.

In each world, men freely choose each act and freely respond to all persuasive measures of God. In any possible world, what each man does, he does freely, which is to say he is not determined regarding any moral choice. That is not to say there are no influences in his life, both natural and supernatural, only that his choice is his choice. God, in His knowledge, knows all things of this world (Is 46:9–11), for this is the world He actualized.

From all possible worlds, God selects the best of all possible worlds to be the world that He will actualize. Once that world is actualized, things will be as they are in that world, and they cannot be otherwise. While creation order establishes how God interacts with any and all possible worlds, the only possible world now is the one God has actualized. The choice to actualize this world is from God's wisdom and goodness, and, therefore, it is the best of all possible worlds. Should anyone object that in another world things would be different for him, the fact is what is true for him today is what he chose freely in this world. Because he might have chosen freely but differently in another world is of no consequence. The best of all possible worlds was not selected on the basis of the state of affairs of one or two individuals, but on the world as a whole. The issue here is that man's moral choice is his own, regardless of what world he is in.

From the possible worlds, God actualizes the world where there is an optimum relationship between good and evil. In terms of salvation, this world is the best world with an optimum balance between those who are saved and those who are lost. This would be in contradistinction to those who say that man's felicity is God's intent and governing principle. However, man's true felicity is dependent on righteousness and peace. Therefore, even if one argues that felicity is God's intended good for man, good must always be understood in terms of the Kingdom of God. In the end, we know that this world is the best of all possible worlds because God pronounced it "very good" (Gen 1:31).

C-O Theodicy in Review

The C-O theodicy begins by describing the two circles of reality and how creation order makes possible an interface between the two. God determines the principles and boundaries governing the relationship between Himself and His creation. This is what I have called the *creation order*, which includes the function and boundaries of both natural and moral ordering. Creation order enables the possibility that the infinite and the finite mind have a meaningful interaction. The infinite personal being is compatible with the finite personal to such a degree that the finite can properly act on behalf of God within created reality. God's creation order is based upon His perfect wisdom, wholly good character and omniscience, and provides the parameters within which and by which He interacts with the world He has actualized. It determines in what ways God will limit the expression of His own attributes within created order, which appears to be necessary for man to be true man. It is necessary in order for man to function as a true rational being in a way that man's choices will have real consequences that will influence, to some degree, the shape of human history where men are neither robots nor totally autonomous. The creation order provides the framework within which man can exercise his God-given power of moral choice while assuring the end will be as God purposed.

Within the structure of the creation order, man can choose good or evil, even where much of the evil turns out to be gratuitous. This is illustrated early in the book of Genesis when Cain kills Abel. There was no greater good from this horrible act. Cain was punished; Adam and Eve undoubtedly grieved. There is no indication that Seth was more righteous than Abel. Cain killing Abel was gratuitous evil, but it did not count against the character of God, nor did it defeat the plan of God.

God's providence works amidst all the evil in this world. Sometimes His providence brings good from the suffering, and other times His work of providence is corrective. Admitting that gratuitous evil exists in this world and arguing that it does not count against God severely weakens the atheist's argument from evil. The most the atheist can argue is that he does not like the structure of the creation order. As an aside, I should say that the C-O theodicy has a strong view of *providence* as defined in this volume. I argue that providence is what keeps everything moving in the right direction in human history, where man is making real choices. I think this is important to point out because those who believe that God determines everything have no need of providence. If everything is determined, then all you need is the will of God, and what God wills must come to pass. So, if everything is determined from the beginning of time, then that is the way it will be—no need of providence.

God's omniscience is understood as including middle knowledge, by which He has actualized the best of all possible worlds. Once this world is actualized, all things remain as they were in its state of potentiality. Based upon His middle knowledge, God selects from all the possible worlds the best possible world. This is a complete world, one that includes all human choices, prayers, answers to prayers, good and bad events, as well as God's promises, commands, interventions (including miracles), and all other matters that make up a possible world. Furthermore, the world encompasses everything from the moment of creation to the final Kingdom state. When it is affirmed that this is the best of all possible worlds, it means that what God created from the beginning was the best it could possibly be. This is not saying that this world is flawless existentially. Under the circumstances, this world is the best both morally and aesthetically in terms of ordering and design. For God to create anything, it would be His best (by choice, and not necessity).

In this world, God uses some evil to bring about good; however, some evil may be gratuitous. The amount of gratuitous evil is at an irreducible minimum in relation to the good, because God knows all the worlds (not actual, but potential worlds—middle knowledge—assuring that the best would be actualized). God decided if He were to create a world (which of necessity is contingent, and, therefore, not morally perfect in the same sense God is) at all (and it seems that it is better to exist than not exist), He selected the one with the least amount of evil as a whole, the least amount of gratuitous evil in particular and the greatest amount of good. There was an optimum balance between the good and evil in general, and, in particular, possibly even an optimum balance between the saved and the unsaved.

As history reveals, man used his power of choice to disobey God and brought sin and death into this world. Man rebelled against his limitedness and chose to disobey God in the hope that He could become like God. Working within the boundaries of creation order, God provided redemption and the assurance of the Kingdom of God on this earth. When God enacted the plan of redemption, He did not create a new man from dust. He worked providentially through the normal procreative process to bring to fruition this redemptive plan. Furthermore, just as it was human choice that brought sin into the world, even so, human choice is involved in man being reconciled to God and delivered from sin and its consequences. God placed two trees in human history and gave commandments concerning both. The fruit of the tree in the Garden came with the command "Eat and die." The fruit of the tree on Calvary comes with the command "Eat and live."

These are examples of God working the plan of redemption within the boundaries of creation order. Furthermore, because sin brought about accidental changes in man and separated him from God, God sent His Spirit to persuade men of their need of Him (Gen 6:3; Jn 16:8–11). God determined the consequences of the disobedience and the consequences of obedience, all of which were a part of creation order. Moreover, the world that was actualized included the entire world (book) that is from creation to the Kingdom.

When taken as a whole, this is the best of all possible worlds even though it contains evil in general and horrific evil in particular. Of this evil, some is moral and some is natural/physical, but it all flows from the fact that because of sin, creation is not like it was intended to be. When believers suffer for righteousness sake, they can know that God is at work for the good of His Kingdom, and they can be encouraged as God administers mercy and comfort for living. When believers suffer because they live in a fallen world, they look to the grace and comfort of God to encourage and strengthen them. Sometimes God delivers *from* and sometimes God delivers *in* the circumstance. In all cases, His grace is sufficient. Because of those who obey God's law, evil and suffering are often prevented so that the events of this world are not as bad as they might be (2 Thess 2:6–7). In addition, there is the common grace of God by which God provides in a general way for His creation (Matt 5:45). All of this is part of God's creation order, which is suggested here as a more adequate way to understand God's relationship to created reality in general and evil in particular.

While this may give the appearance that God has no control, such is not the case. One can see God's control of matters in several ways. First, the direction of human history is shaped in some fashion by God limiting human choices as part of creation order. There are some things that man is not permitted to do from the beginning. Second, God can providentially intervene as He did in Noah's day or as He did at the Tower of Babel. These are cases involving divine intervention where God's intervention is in the name of justice or the welfare of humanity, and does not violate anything He has promised. His providential work assures that gratuitous evil never defeats His plan. Third, God has established the creation order in such a way that human history passes through predetermined points, moving towards a determined end (Is 46:10). There are some events determined by God, and, as such, they form outer boundaries to the possibilities and therefore the direction of human history. Fourth, God can exercise persuasive power to convince men to choose a right course. Consider the salvation of Saul of Tarsus (Acts 9:3–6) or King Nebuchadnezzar (Dan 4:28–37). Fifth, God's answers to prayers are limited in such a way as to direct history. For example, Hezekiah did not get sixteen extra years, only fifteen, and Sodom would have been spared had there been ten righteous persons living in it. Sixth, God works through His people to do that which is consistent with His Kingdom. This is why there are commands for things man is not to do and things he is to do. God's Spirit works through believers to restrain the evil in the world (2 Thess 2:7–8). This is not to say that believers have always acted in this restraining way. There is no doubt, however, that much evil has been restrained by the forces of righteousness, either by believers or unbelievers acting from a Hebrew-Christian worldview.

CONCLUSION

C-O theodicy undoubtedly has its weaknesses. However, I believe that it offers a paradigm shift, which is useful for answering the argument from evil. Instead of making the good that obtains from evil the grounds for God being morally justified in permitting evil, this theodicy focuses on the arrangement necessary for finite beings and the Infinite Being to have a meaningful relationship. In this, the C-O theodicy attempts to avoid what I perceive to be a fatal weakness of the greater-good premise, namely the denial of gratuitous evil. On the practical side, it directs the sufferer's attention to God and His grace in the suffering rather than to the good that might obtain. I believe the Creation-Order theodicy offers not only a better response to the argument from evil, it also provides a stronger theological framework within which one can minister effectively to the needs and questions of those who suffer, especially those with a Christian worldview. In the end, I believe it gives a more coherent response to the question: "God, why this evil?"

NOTES

1. This does not include suffering which may result from justice carried out either by God or man. That type of suffering is not in view in the discussion of evil.
2. I say "certain attributes," since it appears that not all are involved in the same way. For example, it appears that there was no restraint on the love of God or the knowledge of God.
3. This would include notions bound up in what is included in the anthropic principle. The word "harmonious" is not intended to communicate the idea of perfect, only orderly operation.
4. It appears from such texts as Job 39:26–30 that God is dynamically involved in the daily function of creation in general and texts like Genesis 3:8 that God personally interacts with man.

5. When I say "freely made," I am not suggesting that there are no influences acting upon them either mediately or immediately. That is not the type of libertarian freedom (power of moral choice) argued in this book. However, each freely chooses how to respond to other antecedent influences, even though they may have had no choice concerning which influences would be a part of their history. Ultimately, they are accountable for their choices, and, hence, morally responsible.

6. When I say that this is a *natural evil*, I am not suggesting that God was not involved, only that it was an evil within the order of nature.

AFTERWORD

As one who spent 30 years of his life as pastor, I know that one of the most difficult tasks of ministering to people is comforting them in time of suffering. This is true particularly when the suffering appears to be senseless or what is called gratuitous. An example of such senseless suffering is the little girl who was kidnapped, raped and buried alive. It will not do to pretend that somehow this was for some greater good. Nor will it do to romanticize the suffering and death because the little girl was a Christian or say it is okay because you claim little children go to heaven. These responses may be true, but they fail to answer the question of why God *allows* such suffering, not only of that girl, but that of her entire family and community. The responses mentioned only tell us what God might do with the suffering, but not why he allows the suffering and that is the real question.

Over the years I have known the heaviness of soul as I watched good people who loved and believed in God face some of the worst miseries of life. It has been in that context that I wrestled with the Scriptures to find answers to those hard questions. It was through this that I came to my understanding roughly expressed in this book, which admittedly has a philosophical tone to it. Of course, someone might respond by suggesting that people do not want some philosophical discourse, but rather they want answers to soothe the hurting heart. I could not agree more. However, unless one has a coherent framework within which to give that help, one might unintentionally end up saying things not true of God or His ways. I think of it in this way. When someone has cancer and she goes to an oncologist, she probably does not want to hear a lecture on the pathology of cancer—she wants a treatment plan that will restore her to health. However, surely, she must believe that the oncologist knows the pathology of cancer which enables him to suggest an effective treatment plan. So it is with the problem of evil. Those of us who deal with the miseries of this broken world must have a firm understanding of the pathology of evil if we are to give meaningful and helpful counsel to those who are suffering.

However we approach this matter, we must not minimize the brokenness of the world, the depths of human suffering, nor misrepresent God's place in all of this. This brokenness is real and it strikes all of us in one way or the other to a lesser or greater degree. One thing I have always sought to do is to face the brokenness of life with a good dose of reality—both for others and myself. I want to be sure that I am being honest with the situation and with the Bible. It seems to me that those who suffer (either directly or indirectly) have the right to ask about the particulars of this brokenness evident in our world that have touched them. Although we may not be able to give an explanation for every detail, we should say enough about suffering in general that applies to their situation in particular.

As I mentioned earlier, I am not talking about when people ask accusatory questions of God. What I am talking about are questions of serious inquiry, believing there are sufficient reasons for what happens. We can be confident that God knows every situation regarding events and people in His creation. Things do not happen randomly and there are answers for those who ask. Again, let me repeat, when I speak of answers, I am not suggesting we can give a satisfactory answer to every little detail, but we can put the suffering in a proper perspective. I would argue that our questions arise precisely because we believe there are answers—answers that the human heart longs to hear. It is Jesus who says we should seek, ask and knock (Matt 7:7).

When I think of answers to questions, I am not thinking of general answers often given which say we must suffer so we can experience God's grace or all suffering is to give God glory. To argue that human suffering is *necessary* to experience the grace of God (or glory) seems beyond the warrant of Scripture. I am not saying that we do not experience God's grace in suffering (or that in comes cases God is glorified), but only that suffering is not *necessary* to experience His grace. What Scripture says about God's grace in suffering takes suffering as a given, not a necessity. Whereas grace is not an essential attribute of God, it is not necessary that man experience it in order to know the fullness of God. Furthermore, there are more than a few Christians who have ignored God's grace in suffering. It is not difficult to find many examples where a believer has suffered intensely, refused God's grace and become bitter, not better.

It seems obvious that human suffering seldom results in some greater good regardless of what sort it is. Sometimes, yes many times, suffering brings heartache and pain without any visible sign of some greater good. In fact, we have biblical examples where the saint suffered without any good consequences (Heb 11:32–38). The Creation-Order (C-O) theodicy attempts to avoid basing counsel to the sufferer on some notion that all suffering is allowed by God to bring about some kind of greater good. That does not mean that some good never obtains, but that is not necessarily why God *allowed* it.

Some Christians may think that a theodicy is not necessary because it is only theoretical. They long for something practical. They are right on that count. They err, however, in thinking that there is no relationship between the theory and practice. The fact is that any theory without practical application is of little value to humanity. The practical value of answers given will be determined by how true to a Christian view of reality the answers are. That requires an understanding of the world in which we find ourselves as well as some knowledge of how God works in space and time. Without this, our answers can prove to be weightless as long term help to the hurting. In fact, superficial responses have often either minimized or romanticized the suffering and at least tacitly suggested that one should not grieve. The point being that, after all, God is doing something greater in your life, so why grieve.

I think a much more damaging effect of the repose of the greater-good approach, however, is that it ends up affirming that the evil was God's will. While some may try to avoid this conclusion, it is impossible if one is consistent with the greater-good response. It seems to me that at this point it becomes subversive to reasonable men to lead a person to look to God for comfort if it is God's will that has brought the suffering into your life—that is it is for His glory. After all, if it is God's will that the evil come to you for some greater good, then it is best to just "buck up" and take it like a man. In others words, simply say that I will accept it because it is God's will no matter how much it hurts and leaves me empty.

When confronted with the logical conclusion of this position regarding the will of God, many respond by saying that it is the permissive will of God, not His sovereign will (perfect will) that accounts for this evil. If this is true, then how do we escape some disturbing conclusions? First, if it is God's sovereign will that man not murder man, why does His permissive *will* allow it? Second, how many wills does God have and which one seems strongest? Since murder occurs it must be that the permissive will is stronger than the sovereign will. If His permissive will is stronger than His sovereign will, how can one be assured that the sovereign will prevail in the end?

Furthermore, if the evil has all been allowed for my good (or some other God-ordained good such as the glory of God) then I should rejoice that it has come my way. Does it not sound a little strange in light of God's love to say that I should rejoice that my three-year-old was raped and murdered? In such cases, Christians who try to live with this explanation often spend much of their time trying to find the good instead of looking to God's comfort and mercy. Of course the question remains, how much good is required to offset this evil? Furthermore, looking for the good means that one seeks to find consolation not in God, but in the good that obtains because of the suffering. This seems not only futile but biblically wrong-headed. Moreover, when the good is not forthcoming, Christians often become bitter towards God or life, and their spiritual life declines miserably.

According to the C-O theodicy, when a Christian suffers there are several questions to ask. This is to see if it is possible to determine what might be the cause of the suffering. There are several possibilities. One would be because of living righteously and, as a consequence, the person is persecuted for his Christianity. A second could be that, as a Christian, he is living unrepentantly in open sin and God could be disciplining his (Heb 12:5–11). A third reason could be because he lives in a fallen world where things are terribly out of joint (this would include suffering as a consequence of Satan's activity). If it is the first or third, then he should look to God and His mercy for help and comfort, knowing that the evil intent will not prosper against him since it will be tempered by the providential hand of the loving, omnipotent heavenly Father (Matt 5:11,12) and knowing that nothing can separate him from God (Ro 8:38–39). If it is the second, then the Christian should confess his sin and purpose in his heart to forsake the sin by the power of God working in him (1 Jn 1:9; Rom 6:11–13). Should it be the third, he should look to God for strength and grace (2 Cor 1:3–4, 12:9), while being comforted, knowing that in the next phase of this world suffering will be abolished (Rev 21:4).

In the end, should good come from the evil, he can thank God and maximize that good. In all cases he can know that this world is guided by a creation order designed and sustained by an all-wise, all-good and all-powerful God—this is the best of all *possible* worlds. It is better to have this world than not have this world. God is in control (not in the sense that He determines everything but that He knows all things and is providentially involved in the lives of humans) and His Kingdom will come. What He began in Genesis 1 will be completed in spite of the evil that has made its way into this creation. One day, redeemed persons will enjoy what God intended for Adam and Eve, and it will be enjoyed forever. However, there is no assurance that good will come. The fact is, some evil has no purpose, in fact, much of the evil has no purpose. In light of that, such evil/suffering is called gratuitous. However, as I have shown, gratuitous evil does not count against either God's sovereignty or His moral goodness. Because of this, we can encourage the sufferer to look to God for mercy and comfort, knowing God is not indifferent to the suffering.

In addition, I do believe that God in some way suffers with us. When the little girl is raped and buried alive, I believe God weeps. He is not indifferent to our suffering. In fact the Psalmist says that He puts our tears in a bottle (Ps 56:8). When I counsel the suffering, I am apt to tell the individual that God is weeping, as it were, with them. This does seem to be the heart of God as I see Him weeping outside the tomb of Lazarus (Jn 11:35–36). If God is not indifferent in such suffering, then it is most reasonable that He in some way ministers to the person suffering, be it a child or an adult.

I am reminded of what Lewis wrote in *The Magician's Nephew*. You may remember that Digory had inadvertently brought the White Witch to Narnia and Aslan tells him that he now must do something as a consequence. Digory, whose mother was desperately ill, thought for a moment that he might bargain with Aslan that he would do what was necessary if Aslan would do something for his mother. However, he realized immediately that Aslan was not the kind of person with whom one strikes a bargain. So, he agrees to do what Aslan asks. After that, he blurts out:

> "But please, please—won't you—can't you give me something that will cure Mother?" Up till then he had been looking at the Lion's great feet and the huge claws on them; now, in his despair, he looked up at its face. What he saw sur-

prised him as much as anything in his whole life. For the tawny face was bent down near his own and wonder of wonders great shining tears stood in the Lion's eyes. They were such big, bright tears compared with Digory's own that for a moment he felt as if the Lion must really be sorrier about his Mother than he was himself. "My son, my son," said Aslan. "I know, Grief is great."[1]

I think C. S. Lewis got it right on this matter.

At this point, I would like to speak of the suffering of children, which to me is the most emotion-creating of all suffering. In Matthew 18:10, Jesus says regarding little children, "Take heed that you do not despise one of these little ones, for I say to you that in heaven their angels always see the face of my Father who is in heaven." While some may take little ones to refer generally to all believers because they must become as little children, in the early part of the text, the subject is clearly little children. So whatever else this may mean, it seems to me that children have a special place in the economy of God.

Consider for example the story in Genesis 21 which contains the story of Hagar fleeing Abraham's house with Ishmael. Apparently she headed south towards Egypt but as she journeyed, their supply of water ran out. Realizing they would both die, Hagar places the boy under a shrub and goes a bowshot away saying: "Let me not see the death of the boy" (vs. 16). She then "lifted up her voice and wept" (vs. 16). Now what surprises us is in the next verse the text reports:

> And God heard the voice of the lad; and the angel of God called to Hagar out of heaven, and said unto her, What aileth thee, Hagar? fear not; for God hath heard the voice of the lad where he is. Arise, lift up the lad, and hold him in thine hand; for I will make him a great nation. And God opened her eyes, and she saw a well of water; and she went, and filled the bottle with water, and gave the lad drink (vs. 17–19, KJV).

I think it should not be lost on us that it was the lad that God responded to and not the mother. It seems to me that this is consistent with the words of Jesus quoted earlier. My conclusion is that children have a special place in the creation of God. I do not know precisely how this works out in every situation, but I think God intervenes in some way when children suffer, and if we dare make much of David's comment about his dead son, it seems the child goes to heaven. But beyond that, I think God is somehow involved in comforting and aiding the child who suffers.

Lastly, I would like to submit a brief discussion regarding suffering in general. Today, there is a growing belief that the goal of science is to remove all suffering at all costs. Americans have come to demand the absence of suffering at any cost. Consequently, moral boundaries are being pushed to the limits, and beyond, in the name of science's quest for eliminating suffering from the human experience. This goal rests on two erroneous assumptions. The first is the cause of suffering and disease. Science sees these as only a biological/chemical issue when in fact they are a spiritual issue. Death and disease came into the world by sin. The second assumption is that suffering is without redemptive value. If one believes that the elimination of suffering is an absolute in itself, then any means will be acceptable to that end. Consequently, even basic morality can be set aside in the interest of eliminating suffering. While it is legitimate to fight against the fall, it is not to be done outside basic moral boundaries. Surely, no one wants to suffer. To eliminate as much suffering as morally possible is desirable. But one must not assume that suffering has no value. This is not a greater-good idea as I am not speaking now of why God allows evil, but rather how He might use evil/suffering in our lives. Suffering that cannot be eliminated does not mean that the sufferer has no profit from his suffering.

There are several important lessons to be learned from suffering. While lessons can be learned otherwise, suffering makes the point more personal and, hence, sometimes more effective. Suffering is an undeniable and undesirable reality because on this side of final redemption sin produces death. Even Jesus suffered and, remember, the servant is not greater than his Lord. Suffering instructs us in our own mortality (Job 1:20–22). Suffering can teach us to depend on God and His grace (Ps 73:1–2, 21–26; 2 Cor 12:9; Ps 23:4). Suffering also helps us to see the value of God's Word (Ps 119:50, 67, 71). Suffering puts us in touch with God's mercy and comfort (2 Cor 1:2–4) and offers an opportunity to experience God's grace and strength (2 Cor. 12:9–10). In addition, suffering has value in building character (Rom 5:1–5; Ja 1:2–4). Such benefits certainly do not provide moral justification for God allowing the suffering; however, when suffering comes we can benefit spiritually if we look to God. This does not explain why God allowed the suffering, but it does mean that we can rise above the victim mentality and use the event, trusting God in a unique way as did Job and Paul.

In the end, the C-O theodicy offers an alternative way to look at suffering/evil in this world. It suggests that the one suffering look to God who is the God of all comfort and the Father of all mercy. This is instead of trying to find some greater good as a way to justify why God allowed the suffering. In addition, it does not require that all suffering be the will of God allowed in order to teach us some lesson. Nor does it necessarily require that the suffering was allowed by God to bring some greater good as it affirms that gratuitous evil is a reality. That does not mean that all suffering is gratuitous, only that gratuitous evil exists. Also the C-O theodicy does not affirm that all suffering is allowed in order to bring God glory. That is not to say that God may not receive glory by the way the sufferer handles the suffering, but that is quite a different matter altogether. The main point is that gratuitous evil does not count against God's sovereignty or His moral goodness. In this, the sufferer sees God, not as an indifferent Person but One who enters into our suffering with us, desiring to comfort us until that Day when He will wipe away all tears and abolish death forever.

NOTES

1. C. S. Lewis. The Magician's Nephew (New York: Collier Books Edition, 1970),
    142.

APPENDIX
SOME DIFFICULT BIBLICAL TEXTS
ON GOD AND EVIL

In the previous chapters I addressed certain biblical passages relevant to the question of God and evil. I did not, however, consider all the texts common to the larger discussion. Therefore, here I will respond to some of the passages that might seem to contradict the Creation-Order theodicy or appear to make God a moral monster. It is not my intention for this to be an exhaustive treatment either in terms of exegesis or in terms of scope. Instead, I wish to give a general idea how one might respond to either of the above mentioned concerns. Still, I believe the answers given are rational and coherent even though they serve only as possible answers in some cases. Furthermore, I believe the answers are consistent with trinitarian theism, the Bible as a whole, and the Creation-Order (C-O) theodicy.

I begin with an observation regarding how Christians (or any person who wishes to be intellectually honest with the Christian religion) should approach perceived difficult texts such as those associated with God and evil. What must be recognized at once is that these particular difficulties do not entail a logical contradiction. In addition, the Bible as a whole presents God as loving, just, gracious and longsuffering (among other characteristics). All of the texts which raise questions are, in fact, exceptions to the revealed general work of God among humanity. I suggest that what we have in such texts are simply difficulties originating from our human perspective, but that they are not entries that defeat the claim of God's moral perfection.

When the Bible is taken as a whole, it is just as reasonable to think that in the exception texts, God has good and sufficient reasons for acting as He has because He is a perfect moral being. That is to say, we may not know all the reasons, but if God is God, then we can simply say from the beginning that God has His reasons which are totally consistent with His perfect moral being.

Whereas the overwhelming content of the Bible presents God as a morally just God (consider the Father sending His Son to be the savior of the world as the quintessential manifestation of this moral justice and love), it seems unreasonable to conclude that a few difficult texts are sufficient to overthrow belief in God. Of course this would not be the case if such texts entailed a logical contradiction, which in fact they do not. Hence, if there is no logical contradiction and it is only a matter of difficulty in understanding, then what is left is to seek to increase our understanding and not give up our belief in God. If this is a reasonable approach, then it seems to me it is a fair task to posit possible answers which could explain why a particular act is totally consistent with the moral nature of God.

I believe this position is strengthened by what the Bible claims for itself. The Scriptures say "that every word of God is pure" (Prov 30:5) and Jesus said that the Old Testament was the very Word of God (Mk 7:6–13). Given this is what the Bible claims for itself, it seems rather strange that matters otherwise unknowable to man would be inserted in the narrative text which give the appearance of challenging other statements in the Bible. When I say "unknowable" I mean that it is a piece of information that would not otherwise be known to us unless it was revealed in the Bible.

As we shall see, several of the difficult texts are ones that tell us God's mind or motive in a particular event for His particular action. What is instructive is that this is something we would not have known had it not been revealed by the biblical writer. So, if that piece of information were to create a contradiction with other claims about God, it would seem counterproductive to the Bible's claim of accuracy to include such in the narrative. It could be left out and no one would be the wiser. However, because it is included, I believe it is strong evidence for the conclusion that God had morally sufficient reason(s) for the particular act. Although those reasons are not given, the act itself is not inconsistent with who God is. If I am right on this, then I think we should expect it is possible to give plausible explanations as we begin with the assumption there is no final conflict between who God is and what God does—even in the difficult texts. Given that position, I will now attempt some plausible explanations.

The first text under consideration is Joshua 6:21 as viewed in light of Deuteronomy 7:1–4, 16, and 24. Joshua 6 records that Joshua and company "utterly destroyed all that was in the city [Jericho], both man and woman, young and old, ox and sheep and donkey, with the edge of the sword." This is reasonably understood as an act of obedience to God's command in Deuteronomy 7 regarding what Israel should do upon entering the Land. Deuteronomy 7:2 says, "you shall utterly destroy them," however, as we read the text further, it seems to explain what that means: "But thus you shall deal with them; you shall destroy their altars; and break down their sacred pillars; and cut down their wooden images, and burn their carved images with fire" (vs. 5). In verse four of the same chapter Israel was warned not to marry women from the inhabitants of the Land. Furthermore, Israel was not to enter into covenant with them. This seems to give some help in understanding what it meant to destroy completely or utterly—that is, it was to include even the objects of idol worship so that they would not remain as a snare to Israel. In other words, God's concern is that Israel not in any way be influenced to engage in the idolatry of those they were to destroy.

It seems that such a command as found in Deuteronomy 7 and carried out in Joshua 6 seems unloving and brutal to kill even the children. The question that immediately comes to mind is—why? Why would God require such complete removal of all and everything in this *localized* situation? If we begin with the notion that God is just and compassionate as stated in many places and demonstrated on many occasions, our first thought would not be that God is a cruel monster. What would first come to mind is that as God, He must have had good and sufficient moral reasons in this situation. Furthermore, let us remember this is not the normal way God interacts with humanity, but only in cases of what appears to be extreme moral decadence as in the case of Sodom and Gomorrah and in Noah's time.

When Genesis 15:16 is brought into the discussion, it seems apparent that this act of utter destruction is tied to the state of iniquity which had grown to such proportions that this move was necessary to the well being of humanity in general and Israel's in particular. The Genesis text explains why Abram could not have the Land at that time but would need to wait 400 years. The reason given was because "the iniquity of the Amorites is not yet complete" (Gen 15:16). In order for Abram to have the Land presently occupied by others, it was necessary to wait until the present inhabitants could be removed justly. For this a waiting period of 400 years was required of Abram. The indication of the text is this waiting period had something to do with the moral state of those in the Land.

Therefore, it is reasonable to conclude that the moral state of the people living particularly in Jericho had reached a place of such degradation that destruction was just. Destruction of this nature would parallel that of Sodom and Gomorrah earlier in the Genesis record. In fact, these two events do provide a moral paradigm for God's similar action in future cases of similar destruction. If this is right, it helps in understanding what happens at Jericho. The difference between Jericho and Sodom and Gomorrah is that in the former Joshua serves as God's hand of justice whereas in the latter, it is the direct work of God. Furthermore, we know from the testimony of Rahab that there had been sufficient warning from God for Jericho. She says:

> "For we have heard how the LORD dried up the water of the Red sea for you, when ye came out of Egypt; and what ye did unto the two kings of the Amorites, that were on the other side Jordan, Sihon and Og, whom ye utterly destroyed. And as soon as we had heard these things, our hearts did melt, neither did there remain any more courage in any man, because of you: for the LORD your God, he is God in heaven above, and in earth beneath" (Josh 2:10 – 11, KJV).

We see the same is true in God's destruction of Sodom and Gomorrah where we are told that God would have spared it for ten righteous and then does deliver Lot and his family (Gen 18:23–19:1–29). A review of the destruction in Noah's day reveals the same truth, namely that God in His grace provides men with ample warning before there is destruction. We are told that Noah was a preacher of righteousness (2 Pet 2:5), that God had been longsuffering in those days (1 Pet 3:20) and before Noah there was Enoch who also preached repentance and judgment (Jude 14–15).

Here the evidence is clear in all the cases of this type of destruction that God was just in His action, whether directly or by the hand of another. There was sufficient knowledge of God for people in each case to turn to God and leave their immoral lifestyle. In the case of Noah, he and his family are saved; in the case of Lot, he and his family are saved; and in the case of Rahab, she and her family are saved. There is more than sufficient evidence to account for the destruction of Jericho as a just act of God. On the other hand, there is insufficient evidence to convict God as being either immoral or unjust. In conclusion, it seems as reasonable to conclude that God was morally justified in this command.

A second text that often appears in the discussion is Exodus 4:11. Here God says to Moses: "Who has made man's mouth? Or who makes the mute, the deaf, the seeing, or the blind? Have not I, the Lord?" This text only says that God has the power to do this, not that He is the direct cause of all blindness or deafness or that every instance of such is God's direct work. The point is that, if Moses had a speech defect, God was able to overcome it since He has that kind of power. He can overcome birth defects should He so choose. One must take the entirety of Scripture when discerning the meaning, not just one text by itself, as individual statements are always to be understood in the context of the whole. Each individual text does not keep telling us everything about God, it is expected we remember what other texts say. Trying to understand a particular text just by parsing the verbs and defining the nouns is insufficient to determine the meaning of the text.

The 1 Samuel 15:2–3 text is also often quoted as grounds for dismissing God as the most perfect being. The text contains a direct command of God which does not seem to be related to moral decadence as in the case of Jericho:

> Thus saith the LORD of hosts, "I remember that which Amalek did to Israel, how he laid wait for him in the way, when he came up from Egypt. Now go and smite Amalek, and utterly destroy all that they have, and spare them not; but slay both man and woman, infant and suckling, ox and sheep, camel and ass" (KJV).

Here, we learn that this destruction had something to do with Amalek's attack on Israel when it was defenseless. As the story unfolds, Saul failed to be obedient to this utter destruction and was rebuked by Samuel for his failure in complete obedience. What is interesting, however, is that Saul warns the Kenites to get out of the area because he did not want them to be collateral damage in this battle. Here we see the justice of God because the Kenites were not under judgment from God. We see the same pattern here as in the other events just reviewed—the justice and grace of God is evident.

What do we make of this? In this case as with Jericho and Sodom and Gomorrah the group involved in the destruction is limited and specific. However, at least from the text we cannot argue that the destruction of Amalek was the result of some moral degeneracy. Destruction was to come to them for something that had happened some years before. This is one text for which I think we have no other answer than to trust the character of God. We might conclude that moral degradation was the cause of the earlier mistreatment of Israel, but that would seem to go beyond the warrant of the text. Therefore, it seems reasonable to conclude that God was just in requiring it. As with Abraham we say: "Shall not the Judge of all the earth do right?" (Gen 18:25).

As mentioned earlier, if we begin with the assumption that God is a perfect moral being (that is what it means to be God), then when we read of such events in the Old Testament, it is rational to believe that the moral God has good and sufficient reason for what He requires. We must look at all the Bible to see what sort of God with whom we are dealing—a God who is kind and gives much opportunity for believing on Him long before there is any judgment. And when judgment comes, it is never capricious or arbitrary.

In 2 Samuel 12:14ff we find another episode where an act attributed to God at first leaves us in the questioning mode. This passage records the death of David's first son by Bathsheba who was conceived by an act of adultery. It must be remembered that this was a unique situation and not normative which is to say, not every child conceived by an act of adultery was stricken ill by God.

We learn from the report that in this case God wanted David and those who would follow to know that this was the Lord's doing and not just a consequence of living in a fallen world. Otherwise, there would have been no mention of this as God's doing and one would have assumed that the sickness of the child was only a matter of living in a fallen world. The explanation from God is:

> "Howbeit, because by this deed [adultery] thou hast given great occasion to the enemies of the LORD to blaspheme, the child also that is born unto thee shall surely die." And Nathan departed unto his house. And the LORD struck the child that Uriah's wife bare unto David, and it was very sick. . . . And it came to pass on the seventh day, that the child died (2 Sam 12:14 – 15, 18, KJV).

The text is clear, or so it seems to me, that the illness and ultimate death of this child was an event caused directly by God. Furthermore, the reason seems to be that David's sin with Bathsheba gave the enemies of God a point on which to ridicule David's God. If David was a man after God's own heart, how did committing adultery fit into that—it didn't. The enemies of God could have claimed that David's God was no different than the gods of David's enemies.

From our perspective this seems to be a case of God punishing the child for the sin of the parent. However, it may be less a punishment than it is a testimony that one cannot violate the moral laws of God's creation without consequences. This is highlighted in this case as the violation is committed by a high profile leader who claims to be a follower of God. So rather than this event showing that God is not a moral being, it shows just the opposite—He is a moral being who acts justly.

Another point that is instructive is what happens further on the in story. After the child dies, David leaves off his weeping and fasting which rather surprises the servants. When questioned about his behavior, David replied:

> "While the child was yet alive, I fasted and wept: for I said, 'Who can tell whether God will be gracious to me, that the child may live? [23]But now he is dead, wherefore should I fast? Can I bring him back again? I shall go to him, but he shall not return to me'" (2 Sam 12:22 – 23, KJV).

This seems to indicate the child went to heaven.

The question we must ask ourselves is why we are told that the death of the child was the work of God. While God obviously has the power to take life and as Creator has authority over life, He never acts in an arbitrary or capricious manner. It is not possible for God to act in that manner since this would require a change in His essential nature which would mean He would cease to be God. This is impossible, however, as God cannot change God.

It is also instructive that from the perspective of David and those of that time, no question was raised about God's character on this matter. Their view of God meant that God could be trusted and if He did something like this, He had good and sufficient reasons. Furthermore, it is instructive to point out that the reason given for God's interference in taking the child's life was so that everybody would know that He is the true God of Israel—the only true God. So, this act was not to call God's moral being into question, but quite the contrary, it was to establish that fact.

Furthermore, if it were common knowledge that the death of all children was the immediate work of God, there would be no need to tell David this was the work of God. Therefore, we can conclude this was a special situation of God's intervention for which God had good and sufficient reasons. Furthermore, we have no justification to assume that when a child dies that it is God's doing unless God speaks to us as He did David.

We may not understand all the factors involved in this case, but the overwhelming evidence in Scripture is that God is not a capricious God. Therefore, we reasonably conclude that God has sufficient reason in acting in this way on this occasion. I can see no reason why such an incident should lead us to overthrow everything else we know about God and His gracious intervention with humanity.

One last text from the Old Testament is the book of Job. The first chapter of Job gives us the context within which to understand what follows. At the beginning we are told that Job was "blameless and upright, and one who feared God and shunned evil" (Job 1:1). Whatever the story is about, it is not about some hidden sin or open sin, such as pride in Job's life, as the Divine assessment of this man is that he is "blameless and upright." We learn a little later on in the first chapter that Satan comes before God where we listen in on an ongoing conversation between God and Satan. We pick up the dialogue in verse eight:

> And the LORD said unto Satan, "Hast thou considered my servant Job, that there is none like him in the earth, a perfect and an upright man, one that feareth God, and escheweth evil?" Then Satan answered the LORD, and said, "Doth Job fear God for nought? Hast not thou made an hedge about him, and about his house, and about all that he hath on every side? Thou hast blessed the work of his hands, and his substance is increased in the land. But put forth thine hand now, and touch all that he hath, and he will curse thee to thy face" (Job 1:8 – 11, KJV).

What takes place after this is clear. God gives Satan a limited range of possible ways to harm Job, except the taking of his life. What happens in the next chapter is the record of Satan's striking out against Job, taking everything from him except his wife and his own life. It is in this state of affairs we find Job in chapter three, sitting in an ash heap tormented by boils all over his body, and of course, the vexing counsel of his three friends. As a qualifier, here I do not offer a complete commentary on Job, but only point to what I think are essential parts to the story relative to suffering.

First and importantly, we have a summary statement by God that "In all this Job did not sin nor charge God with wrong" (Job 1:22). At the end of the story, God says: "And so it was, after the Lord had spoken these words to Job, that the Lord said to Eliphaz the Temanite, "'My wrath is aroused against you and your two friends, for you have not spoken of Me what is right, as My servant Job has'" (Job 42:7). Some might say (and I have heard it said) that Job was out of line pushing God for an answer regarding all that had befallen him. The text, however, tells a different story; it was not a self-righteous attitude on Job's part that caused him to ask the questions because God says in all of this he did not sin. Yes, Job did press God for answers, but it was not considered wrong and it seems to me that it is poor exegesis to conclude anything but that from the text.

Job confesses in the middle of this that God can be trusted as he says, "'Though He slay me, yet will I trust Him'" (Job 13:15). Job's question is not about evil in general, but the particulars of his own situation. However, he does not get an answer because Job's suffering is related to the angelic conflict. We know this from the first chapter. It is likely that had such information have been given to Job, it would have been beyond his understanding at that time.

It is true that in this case (as in many of our sufferings) it turns out in the end that Job has to trust God for what lies beyond human understanding (not contrary to human understanding). Of course it was not that no one would ever know, but at this point in time Job was not to know. Furthermore, we must not think that the book of Job explains all suffering in the world as that would be placing much more weight on this text than is warranted.

What was really going on in the book of Job was the great cosmic struggle between light and darkness at the cosmic level. The book is not about Job's pride or some sin God was trying to root out of his life. It is about whether Job loved God only because God put a hedge about him and increased his wealth (Job 1:10). Here in the book of Job, that question is answered once and for all and Satan loses his accusation against God that men only love God because God treats them so lavishly. Apparently from the language of the early chapters, Job was a test case.

This book is about a charge against God (from Satan), not against Job. What we see in this book is a man who really struggles with God openly and God honors that by engaging Job fairly. God does not tell Job anything new, but helps him to remember what he already knew about God and who He is (Job 42:5). However, God deemed it inappropriate (or for some other reason) that in this case it would not be in Job's best interest to know precisely what was going on—he would have to trust God. Once again, I want to remind the reader that this story should not be used as a paradigm for understanding all suffering in this world.

I offer one final text for our consideration found in the New Testament. The ninth chapter of the Gospel of John we read:

> And as Jesus passed by, he saw a man which was blind from his birth. And his disciples asked him, saying, "Master, who did sin, this man, or his parents, that he was born blind?" Jesus answered, "Neither hath this man sinned, nor his parents: but that the works of God should be made manifest in him" (Jn 9:1 – 3, KJV).

Notice what this is about. It is about a man who had been born blind and there was the assumption that somehow this condition must be connected to some personal sin—at least that was how the disciples saw it. Jesus, however, corrects the view of the disciples and points out they have misunderstood. Jesus informed the disciples that the man was "born" blind, not because of sin, but that the "works of God should be manifest in him."

What Jesus did not say is that God caused or allowed the man to be born blind for God's glory. The cause of his blindness is not addressed. It is reasonable to conclude that the blindness was a manifestation of what sin has done in disrupting the goodness of God's creation.

Jesus focuses on what is about to happen by saying that the man's blindness was from birth so that "the works of God might be revealed." Whereas he was going to be healed by Jesus sometime after he was born, it was possible he could have been healed in the womb. In that case, however, no one would have known that it was God who did it. It is about the works of God being revealed, that is, done before men. This is why he is *born* blind.

There are two issues here; one is the cause of blindness, which Jesus does not answer. All Jesus says is that the disciples are wrong in there assumption that the blindness was caused by some personal sin—either by the man or his parents. The other issue that Jesus addresses is that He must do the work of the Father (vs. 4) while He is in the world as the light of the world (vs. 5). Whereas the blind man would eventually be healed, he could have been healed in the womb, however, no one would have known that it was God's work. That means that the work of God would not be *manifest* in him. Now, he is openly healed as a testimony to who Jesus is—God, with the power to heal.

In conclusion, I believe the biblical evidence is overwhelming that God is a morally perfect being who acts in justice and in love. This is manifest in His sending His Son to die for the sins of the world that we might be reconciled to God and have eternal life (Jn 3:16; 2 Cor 5:18, 19). Therefore, when considering passages which appear at first blush as incongruous with our idea of God, they can be reasonably understood as being consistent with the perfect character of God with further consideration. Therefore, I find charges that God causes evil for His glory or that He either acts Himself or instructs others to act immorally on His behalf to be without persuasive evidence. The fact is, those who would bring such charges against God simply cannot meet the burden of proof. And it is they who must prove God guilty as the presumption is that He is the morally perfect being manifest in all His thoughts and in all His ways.

SELECTED BIBLIOGRAPHY

Abraham, W., 1998, *Canon and Criterion in Christian Theology*, Oxford: Clarendon.

Adams, M. M., 1999, *Horrendous Evils and the Goodness of God*, Ithaca, NY: Cornell University Press.

Adams, R. M. 1987, *The Virtue of Faith*, Oxford: Oxford University Press.

Alston, W. 2004. "Do Mystics See God?" in Contemporary Debates in Philosophy of Religion, ed. by Michael Peterson and Raymond Van Arragon. Oxford: Blackwell, p. 145–58.

——, 1991, *Perceiving God*, Ithaca: Cornell University Press.

——, 1991, "The Inductive Argument from Evil," *Philosophical Perspectives*, 5, 29–68.

Anderson, P.S. 1997, *A Feminist Philosophy of Religion*, Oxford: Blackwell.

Augustine 1972 [426], *The City of God* (translated by H. Bettenson), Harmondsworth: Penguin.

Ayer, A. J. 1973, *The Central Questions of Philosophy*, London: Weidenfeld and Nicolson.

Beaty, M. (ed.) 1990, *Christian Theism and the Problems of Philosophy*, Notre Dame: University of Notre Dame Press.

Beaty, M. and Taliaferro, C., 1990, "God and Concept Empiricism," *Southwest Philosophy Review*, 6:2, 97–105.

Blackwell Clark, B. and Clark, B.R., 1998, *The Philosophy of Religion*, Oxford: Blackwell.

Boyd, Gregory A., 2001, *Satan and the Problem of Evil*, Downers Grove: InterVarsity Press.

Brown, D., 1987, *Continental Philosophy and Modern Theology*, Oxford: Blackwell.

Chappell, T., 1996, "Why is Faith a Virtue?" *Religious Studies* 32, 27–36 .

Craig, W., 1979, *The Kalam Cosmological Argument*, New York: Barnes and Noble.

——, 1980, *The Cosmological Argument from Plato to Leibniz*, New York: Barnes and Noble.

Craig, W. L. and Smith, Q. 1993, *Theism, Atheism, and Big Bang Cosmology*, Oxford: Clarendon Press.

Creel, R., 1995, *Divine Impassibility*, Cambridge: Cambridge University Press.

Davis, C., 1989, *The Evidential Force of Religious Experience*, Oxford: Oxford University Press.

Davies, B., 1993, *An Introduction to the Philosophy of Religion*, Oxford: Oxford University Press.

Dembski, William A., 2009, *The End of Christianity: Finding a Good God in an Evil World*, Nashville: B&H Publishing Group.

——, 2006, *The Reality of God and the Problem of Evil*, London: Continuum.

Dombrowski, D. 2006. Rethinking the Ontological Argument. Cambridge: Cambridge University Press.

Dore, R., 1984, *Theism*, Dordrecht: D. Reidel.

Earmon, J., *Hume's Abject Failure*, Oxford: Oxford University Press.

Evans, S., 1996, *The Historical Christ and the Jesus of Faith: The Incarnational Narrative as History*, Oxford: Clarendon Press.

——, 1985, *Philosophy of Religion*, Downers Grove, IL: Intervarsity.

Everitt, N., 2004, *The Non-Existence of God*, London: Routledge.

Fales, E., 2004. "Do Mystics See God?" in *Contemporary Debates in Philosophy of Religion*, M.Peterson and R. VanArragon (eds). Oxford: Blackwell, 145–57.

Firth, R., 1970: "Ethical Absolutism and the Ideal Observer," in W. Sellars and J. Hospers (eds), *Readings in Ethical Theory*, Englewood Cliffs, NJ: Prentice-Hall, 200–21.

Flew, A., 1984, *God, Freedom and Immortality*, Buffalo: Prometheus Books.

Flew, A. and MacIntyre (eds.), 1995, *New Essays in Philosophical Theoolgy*, New York: Macmillan.

Forrest, P., 1996, *God without the Supernatural*: A *Defense of Scientific Theism*, Ithaca: Cornell University Press.

Foster, J., 1985, *Ayer*, London: Routledge and Kegan Paul.

Geivett, R. Douglas, 1993, *Evil and The Evidence for God*, Philadelphia: Temple University Press.

Geivett, R. Douglas and Sweetman, B. (eds.), 1992: *Contemporary Perspectives on Religious Epistemology*, Oxford: Oxford University Press.

Gellman, J., 1997, *Experience of God and the Rationality of Theistic Belief*, Ithaca: Cornell University Press.

——, 2001, *Mystical Experience of God: A Philosophical Inquiry*. London: Ashgate.

Griffiths, P., 1994, *On Being Buddha*, Albany: State University of New York Press.

Hare, J.E., 1996, The *Moral Gap*, Oxford: Oxford University Press.

Hasker, W., 1989, *God, Time, and Knowledge*, Ithaca: Cornell University Press.

——, 1999, *The Emergent Self*, Ithaca: Cornell University Press.

Helm, P., 1988: *Eternal God*, Oxford: Oxford University Press.

——, 2000, *Faith and Reason*, Oxford: Oxford University Press.

Hempel, C., 1959, "The Empiricist Criterion of Meaning," in *Logical Positivism*, ed. A.J. Ayer, Glencoe, Ill: Free Press.

Hepburn, R.W., 1963, "From World to God", *Mind*, 72, 40–50.

Hick, J., 1978, *Evil and the God of Love*, New York: Harper and Row.

——, 1973, *God and the Universe of Faiths*, London: Macmillan.

——, 1989, *An Interpretation of Religion: Human Responses to the Transcendent*, New Haven, CT: Yale University Press.

——, 1990, *Philosophy of Religion* (4th ed.), Englewood Cliffs, NJ: Prentice-Hall.

——, 1966, *Rational Theistic Belief without Proof*, London and Basingstoke: Macmillan.

——, (ed.) 1970, *Classical and Contemporary Readings in the Philosophy of Religion*, Englewood Cliffs, NJ: Prentice-Hall.

Hick, J. and McGill, A., (eds.), 1967, *The Many Faced Argument*, New York: Macmillan.

Hill, D., 2005, *Divinity and Maximal Greatness*, London: Routledge.

Howard-Snyder, D. (ed.), 1996, *The Evidential Argument from Evil*, Bloomington: Indiana University Press.

Howard-Snyder, Daniel ed., 1996, *The Evidential Argument from Evil*, Bloomington: Indiana University Press.

Howard-Snyder, Daniel and Moser, P., (eds.), 2001, *Divine Hiddenness*, Cambridge: Cambridge University Press.

Hughes, C., 1989, *On a Complex Theory of a Simple God*, Ithaca: Cornell University Press.

Hughes, G., 1995, *The Nature of God*, London: Routledge.

Hunter, Cornelius G., 2001, *Darwin's God: Evolution And The Problem Of Evil*, Ada, MI: Brazos Press.

Jordan, J., 1994, *Gambling on God: Essay's on Pascal's Wager*, Lanham, MD: Rowman & Littlefield.

Kenny, A., 1979, *The God of the Philosophers*, Oxford: Clarendon Press.

Kerr, F., 1988, *Theology after Wittgenstin*, Oxford: Blackwell.

Kvanvig, J., 1986, *The Possibility of an All-Knowing God*, London: Macmillan.

Kwan, Kai-man., 2003. "Is the Critical Trust Approach to Religious Experience Incompatible with Religious Particularism? *Faith and Philosophy* 20:2, 152–169.

Leftow, B., 1991, *Time and Eternity*, Ithaca: Cornell University Press.

Leslie, J., 1989, *Universes*, London: Routledge.

MacDonald, S., 1991, *Being and Goodness*, Ithaca: Cornell University Press.

Mackie, J., 1985, *The Miracle of Theism*, Oxford: Clarendon Press.

Malcolm, N., 1975, "The Groundlessness of Religious Beliefs", in S. Brown (ed.), *Reason and Religion*, Ithaca: Cornell University Press, 143–157.

Martin, M., 1990, *Atheism*, Philadelphia: Temple University Press.

Meynell, H., 1982, *The Intelligible Universe*, New York: Barnes and Noble.

Middelmann, Udo, 2007, *The Innocence of God*, Colorado Springs: Paternoster Publishing.

Mitchell, B. (ed.), 1971, *The Philosophy of Religion*, Oxford: Oxford University Press.

——, 1973, *The Justification of Religious Belief*, London: Macmillan.

——, 1994, *Faith and Criticism*, Oxford: Oxford University Press.

Morris, T.V., 1991, *Our Idea of God*, Downers Grove: InterVarsity.

——, 1986, *The Logic of God Incarnate*, Ithaca: Cornell University Press.

——, 1987: *Anselmian Explorations*. Notre Dame: University of Notre Dame Press.

Morris, T. V. (ed.), 1987, *The Concept of God*, Oxford: Oxford University Press.

Nielsen, K., 1996, *Naturalism Without Foundations*, Buffalo: Prometheus Press.

O'Conner, David, 1998, *God and Inscrutable Evil*, New York: Rowman & Littlefield Publishers.

Oppy, Graham, 2006, *Arguing About Gods*, Cambridge: Cambridge University Press.

——, 1995, *Ontological Arguments and Belief in God*, Cambridge: Cambridge University Press.

Padgett, A., 1992, *God, Eternity and the Nature of Time*, New York: St. Martin's Press.

Penelhum, T., 1983, *God and Skepticism*, New York: Springer.

——, 1989, *Faith*, New York: Macmillan.

Peterson, Michael, 1998, *God and Evil*, Boulder, CO: Westview Press.

——, 1992, *The Problem of Evil: Selected Readings*, Notre Dame: University of Notre Dame Press.

——, et al., 1991, *Introduction to the Philosophy of Religion*, Oxford: Oxford University Press.

Peterson, M., Hasker, W., Reichenbach, B., and Basinger, D. (eds.), *Philosophy of Religion: Selected Readings*, Oxford: Oxford University Press.

Phillips, D. Z., 1966, *Concept of Prayer*, New York, Schocken Books.

——, 1976, *Religion Without Explanation*, Oxford: Blackwell.

——, 2005, *The Problem of Evil and the Problem of God*, Minneapolis: Augsburg Fortress Publishers.

Pike, Nelson, 2002, *God and Timelessness*, Wipf and Stock Publishers.

Plantinga, A., 1967, *God and Other Minds*, Ithaca: Cornell University Press.

——, 1974, *The Nature of Necessity*, Oxford: Oxford University Press.

——, 1980, *Does God Have a Nature?*, Milwaukee: Marquette University Press.

——, 1993, *Warrant: the Current Debate*, Oxford: Oxford University Press.

——, 1993, *Warrant and Proper Function*, Oxford: Oxford University Press.

——, 2003, *Warranted Christian Belief*, Oxford: Oxford University Press.

Proudfoot, W., 1976, *God and Self*, Lewisburgh: Bucknell University Press.

——, 1985, *Religious Experience*, Berkeley: University of California Press.

Putnam, Hilary, 1983, *Realism and Reason: Philosophical Papers*, Vol.3, Cambridge: Cambridge University Press.

Reichenbach, B., 1972, *The Cosmological Argument*, Springfield, IL: Thomas Press.

——, 1982, *Evil and a Good God*. New York: Fordham University Press.

Rescher, N., 1985, *Pascal's Wager*, Notre Dame: University of Notre Dame Press.

Rhees, R., 1969, *Without Answers*, New York: Schocken Books.

Rowe, W., 1993, *Philosophy of Religion*, Belmont: Wadsworth.

——, ed., 2001, *God and the Problem of Evil*, Malden, MA: Blackwell Publishers, Inc.

——, 1971, *The Cosmological Argument, Princeton, NY: Princeton University Press.*

Rundle, B., 2004, *Why There is Something Rather Than Nothing*, Oxford: Oxford University Press.

Schellenberg, J., 2005, *Prolegomena to Philosophy of Religion*, Ithaca: Cornell University Press.

Schlesinger, G., 1977, *Religion and Scientific Method*, Dordrecht: Reidel.

——, 1988, *New Perspectives on Old-Time Religion*, New York: Oxford University Press.

Schwarz, Hans, 1995, *Evil: A Historical and Theological Perspective,* trans. Mark Worthing, Minneapolis: Fortress Press.

Sessions, L., 1994, *The Concept of Faith: A Philosophical Investigation*, Ithaca: Cornell University Press.

Sharma, A., 1990, *A Hindu Perspective on the Philosophy of Religion*, New York: St. Martin's Press.

Smart, J.J.C. and Haldane, J.J., 1996, *Atheism and Theism*, Oxford: Blackwell.

Smart, N., 1986, "Religion as a Discipline?" in *Concept and Empathy*, ed. D. Wiebe, New York: New York University Press, 157–162.

Sobel, J., 2004, *Logic and Theism*, Cambridge: Cambridge University Press.

Sorensen, R. A., 1992, *Thought Experiments*, Oxford: Oxford University Press.

Soskice, J. M., 1984, *Metaphor and Religious Language*, Oxford: Oxford University Press.

Stiver, D., 1996, *The Philosophy of Religious Language*, Oxford: Blackwell.

Swinburne, R., 1977, *The Coherence of Theism*, Oxford: Clarendon Press.

——, 1979, *The Existence of God*, Oxford: Clarendon Press.

——, 1983, *Faith and Reason*, Oxford: Clarendon.

——, 1986, *The Evolution of the Soul*, Oxford: Clarendon.

——, 1994, *The Christian God*, Oxford: Clarendon.

——, 1996, *Is There a God?*, Oxford: Oxford University Press.

——, 1998, *Providence and the Problem of Evil*, Oxford: Oxford University Press.

Taliaferro, C., 1998, *Contemporary Philosophy of Religion*, Oxford: Blackwell.

——, 1994, *Consciousness and the Mind of God*, Cambridge: Cambridge University Press.

——, 2001: "Sensibility and Possibilia: A Defense of Thought Experiments," *Philosophia Christi* 3, 403–402.

——, 2005: *Evidence and Faith: Philosophy of Religion since the seventeenth century.* Cambridge: Cambridge University Press.

Taylor, R., 1963, *Metaphysics*. Englewood Cliffs, NJ: Prentice-Hall.

Tilghman, B.R. 1993, *An Introduction to Philosophy of Religion*, Oxford: Blackwell.

Tracy, T.F. (ed.), 1994, *The God Who Acts*, University Park: Pennsylvania State University Press.

Trigg, R., 1989, *Reality at Risk*, London: Harvester.

——, 1993, *Rationality and Science: Can Science Explain Everything?*, Oxford: Blackwell.

Van Cleve, J., 1999, *Problems from Kant*. Oxford: Oxford University Press.

Van Inwagen, P., 1983, *An Essay on Free Will*, Oxford: Clarendon Press.

——, 2004, *Christian Faith and The Problem of Evil*, Grand Rapids: Wm. B. Eerdmans Publishing Company.

——, 1995, *God, Knowledge and Mystery*, Ithaca: Cornell University Press.

——, 2006, *The Problem of Evil*, Oxford: Oxford University Press.

Wainwright, W., 1981, *Mysticism: A Study of Its Nature, Cognitive Value, and Moral Implications*, Madison: University of Wisconsin Press.

——, 1988, *Philosophy of Religion*, Belmont: Wadsworth.

——, (ed.), 1996, *God, Philosophy, and Academic Culture*, Atlanta: Scholars Press.

Westphal, M., 1984, *God, Guilt, and Death*, Bloomington: Indiana University Press.

Whitehead, A.N., 1978, *Process and Reality*, New York: Free Press.

Wierenga, E., 1989, *The Nature of God*, Ithaca: Cornell University Press.

Wisdom, J., 1944–1945, "Gods," Proceedings of the Aristotelian Society 45, 185–206.

Wright, N.T., 2006, *Evil and the Justice of God*, Downers Grove: InterVarsity Press.

Wolterstorff, N., 1976, *Reason within the Bounds of Religion*, Grand Rapids: Eerdmans.

——, 1982, "God Everlasting" in S. M. Cahn and D. Shatz (eds), *Contemporary Philosophy of Religion*, Oxford: Oxford University Press, 77–98.

Wykstra, S., 1984, "The Humean Obstacle to Evidential Arguments from Suffering", *International Journal for Philosophy of Religion*, 16, 73–93.

Yandell, K., 1993, *The Epistemology of Religious Experience*, Cambridge: Cambridge University Press.

Zagzebski, L.T., 1991, *The Dilemma of Freedom and Foreknowledge*, New York: Oxford University Press.

INDEX

ABOUT THE AUTHOR

Bruce A. Little is professor of Philosophy of Religion and Director of the L. Russ Bush Center for Faith and Culture at Southeastern Baptist Theological Seminary in Wake Forest, North Carolina. He has two earned doctorates and an honorary degree from University of Constantin Brancusi in Targu Jiu, Romania (2007). Since 1995 he has maintained an active apologetic ministry in Eastern Europe where he has been invited by various state universities and schools to present class lectures on a variety of topics within the context of a Christian worldview. In addition his teaching ministry has taken him to Thailand, Malaysia, Norway, Switzerland, Germany, Romania, Czech Republic, Bulgaria, Kenya and Nigeria. He is published in academic journals and is the author of a book titled, *A Creation-Order Theodicy: God and Gratuitous Evil* (University Press of America 2005), the editor of a book with P & R Publishers titled *Francis A Schaeffer: A Mind and Heart for God* (2010), editor of a forthcoming book *Defending the Faith and Engaging Culture: Essays in Honor of Dr. L. Russ Bush* (Broadman & Holman) and has contributed to other books. In addition, he has co-written four books with Russian professors from the Tavrichesky National University in Simferopol, Ukraine.

Dr. Little lives in Wake Forest, North Carolina with his wife Nancy. They have one daughter who is married with two children.

CPSIA information can be obtained at www.ICGtesting.com
260422BV00005B/5/P

9 780761 852544